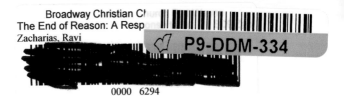

THE
END OF
REA SON

Also by Ravi Zacharias

The Grand Weaver:
How God Shapes Us Through
the Events of Our Lives

The Grand Weaver:
How God Shapes Us Through
the Events of Our Lives
audio

Is Your Church Ready?
Motivating Leaders to Live an Apologetic Life
(general editor with Norman Geisler)

Walking from East to West

Walking from East to West audio

Walking from East to West ebook

Who Made God?
And Answers to Over 100 Other
Tough Questions of Faith
(general editor with Norman Geisler)

THE
END OF
REASON

A RESPONSE TO THE NEW ATHEISTS

RAVI ZACHARIAS

ZONDERVAN®

ZONDERVAN.com/
AUTHORTRACKER
follow your favorite authors

ZONDERVAN®

The End of Reason
Copyright © 2008 by Ravi Zacharias

Requests for information should be addressed to:

Zondervan, *Grand Rapids, Michigan 49530*

Library of Congress Cataloging-in-Publication Data

Zacharias, Ravi K.
    The end of reason : a response to the new atheists / Ravi
  Zacharias.
       p.   cm.
    Includes bibliographical references and index.
    ISBN 978-0-310-28251-8 (hardcover)
    1. Apologetics. 2. Christianity and atheism. I. Title.
  BT1103. Z34   2008
  239'.7 — dc22
                                          2007039358

Published in association with the literary agency of Wolgemuth and Asso-
ciates, Inc.

Interior design by Beth Shagene

Printed in the United States of America

---

08 09 10 11 12 13 • 19 18 17 16 15 14 13 12 11 10 9 8 7 6 5 4 3 2 1

CONTENTS

Foreword / 7

Prologue / 13

The End of Reason / 21

Notes / 129

Subject Index / 137

FOREWORD

Shortly after Sam Harris published his first poison pen letter against religion, *The End of Faith*, I invited him to debate a Christian on my television show. He came into the studio with a swagger, full of the same supreme confidence with which he ridiculed Christianity and other faiths in his book. But during the taping, Christian attorney Hugh Hewitt, piped in via satellite, skewered Harris's inflammatory rhetoric, exposing the book's inconsistencies, recycled arguments, and lapses in logic.

When Harris departed the studio, he looked ashen. His overheated attacks against Christianity might have brought applause in his inbred world of atheism, but I don't think he had ever tried to test them against a well-informed and articulate defender of the Christian faith.

Nevertheless, that didn't stop Harris. He went on to publish a second diatribe against religion,

Letter to a Christian Nation, which again found a ready audience among those who lacked the training to see through its flimsy facade. Together with a wave of other books promoting militant atheism, authored by Richard Dawkins, Daniel Dennett, Christopher Hitchens and others, these books by Harris have confused spiritual seekers and even rocked the faith of some Christians.

The time has come for someone to slay this dragon of disbelief—and I can think of no better person to wield the sword than my friend Ravi Zacharias.

Ravi comes to the task with unique credentials. Himself a former atheist, Ravi personally knows the bankruptcy of living as if there is no God, and thus he is impervious to the false allure of atheism being promoted by this new breed of spiritual iconoclasts.

As an insightful and accomplished philosopher, Ravi is able to systematically dismantle the feeble case for skepticism built by Harris. And as an astute theologian, he is equipped to dispel the falsehoods and misinterpretations of Scripture that fuel Harris's disdain for Christianity.

With relentless logic, an impressive grasp of the relevant literature, a deep understanding of world religions, and an unerring sense of grace and conviction, Ravi manages to unveil the embarrassing impotency of Harris's arguments. As Ravi concludes, the emperor of atheism has no clothes—and none of Harris's frantic efforts can succeed in covering him up.

Unlike Harris, Ravi is willing to take the claims of atheism to their logical conclusions. In fact, Ravi's own despair from atheism once brought him to the brink of personal destruction. Thus he is able to write not merely as a dispassionate observer, but rather as an impassioned champion of the spiritual truth that rescued him from a life of hopelessness and purposelessness.

I also spent much of my early life as a spiritual skeptic. During that time, I tried to be honest about the implications of an atheistic world. I didn't pretend that my atheism would lead to a new era of enlightenment and altruism. I didn't claim that a world without faith in God would somehow be a kinder and gentler place.

Instead, I knew that my atheism was drawing me down a path of narcissism, hedonism, and despondency. Yet I would rather have gone down that ultimately self-destructive road than to manufacture a belief in a phony god who doesn't exist. My attitude was that if atheism represented the best description of reality, then so be it. It didn't give me much to live for or look forward to, but truth is what it is.

In the end, though, I was prompted by my agnostic wife's conversion to Christianity to thoroughly investigate where the evidence of science and history really point. I was utterly stunned by the avalanche of evidence that undergirds Christianity. In my view, the most rational response was to put my trust in Christ. As someone trained in journalism and law, I had no choice but to respond to the facts.

The result has been a series of positive changes in my character, values, morality, priorities, and relationships. Because of my faith in Christ, anyone who knows me would say that I'm a better husband, father, citizen, and person.

Ravi is thoroughly conversant with the evidence for Christianity. In this book, he doesn't just refute Harris, but he also builds an affirmative case for the existence of God. Despite the protestations of Harris, Dawkins, Hitchens, and their ilk, this is where truth resides. There are no answers in atheism.

If you've read any of Harris's attacks on faith, then I urge you to consider Ravi's words with an open mind. Says Proverbs 18:17 (NLT): "The first to speak in court sounds right—until the cross-examination begins." In other words, often when we hear one side of a case presented, the evidence sounds persuasive. But then we hear the other side of the story, and suddenly we see the initial case crumble in the light of new facts and arguments. I suspect that's what you'll experience as you read this book.

So read on, and when you're done, pass along this book to a friend who also has found his or her faith undermined by Harris and his spiritually cynical cronies.

LEE STROBEL, author,
The Case for Christ,
The Case for Faith,
The Case for a Creator, and
The Case for the Real Jesus

PROLOGUE

A university student arrives home and informs his parents that, after reading a popular atheist's book, he has renounced his family's faith. His mother, particularly, is shattered by the news. The father struggles to engage his son in dialogue, but to no avail. The deepening grief causes them to distance themselves from their son. When the game of silence does not work, the mother is plunged further into depression and despair. The grandparents become involved, watching in anguish as beliefs that have been held dear in the family for generations crumble. Before long, this family that was once close and peaceable is now broken and hostile. Abusive words between mother and son are exchanged with increasing frequency and intensity, and the siblings blame their brother's new strident atheism for the rift in the family. After one long night of arguing with her son, pleading unsuccessfully with him to reconsider his position, the mother takes an overdose of prescription medication and ends her life, unable to accept what she interprets to be the destruction of her family.

Although this particular scenario is imaginary, I suspect that in some measure similar scenes have played out more than a few times since the publication of Sam Harris's bestselling *Letter to a Christian Nation*. It is quite possible that many a young man or woman, stirred by the passion and intent of Harris's book, has repudiated the values intrinsically bound up in the belief in God held dear by parents and ancestors long before them.

In 2005, Harris, a doctoral student at Stanford, published the first of two books that are absolutely and unabashedly hostile to all religions—but particularly to the Christian faith. It is time for us as Americans, Harris states in these books, to outgrow our religious beliefs. His unvarnished hatred for things religious is embellished with strong language and illustrations designed to convince the world that Christians in particular really are buffoons or imbeciles for believing in God. I have always found it fascinating how relativists who say they love the idea of tolerance ultimately reveal themselves to be among the most bigoted. So Harris writes to "America" but in fact to the whole world, telling us that science has the answers to our questions about life and that religion is the bane of existence.

But why do I begin to address a work as serious-minded as that of Harris with an imaginary scene like the one above? Because realities that are far from imaginary are enveloped in this story, and I wonder what Harris would say to those possibilities.

He may argue that the grief his book may cause families such as this one is justified and even necessary sometimes if the young student in the story and others like him are going to stop believing and living a lie. Does this sound familiar? He may well justify any amount of grief to any number of people because of an insistence that the value of his "truth" is greater than the destruction of a family. But to do so raises a huge question, doesn't it? If in the microcosm of this one little episode Harris were to justify the devastation he has caused for the sake of what he sees as the truth, why does he deny God the same justification for allowing suffering in all of the intricacies and possibilities of a lifetime?

Harris's biggest complaint against God is that so much suffering is experienced by humanity in the name of God's sovereignty and goodness; yet in his own little world he would, I suspect, turn a blind eye to any incidental pain in order to freely proclaim "liberation" from "falsehood." In a recent interview Bethany Saltman suggested that Harris may have gone too far in some of the things he has said. But he responded by saying that if he had a magic wand with which to eradicate either religion or rape, he would choose to eradicate religion. This strains credulity. I simply pray that none of those he loves are ever raped and come to him for solace. Evidently, while belief in his atheism is worth any price, religious belief is too costly.

This duplicity is only the tip of the iceberg in Harris's belabored tirade against religion. With Christopher Hitchens, Richard Dawkins, and a few others, he is calling for the banishment of all religious belief. "Away with this nonsense" is their battle cry! In return, they promise a world of new hope and unlimited horizons—once we have shed this delusion of God. I have news for them—news to the contrary. The reality is that the emptiness that results from the loss of the transcendent is stark and devastating, both philosophically and existentially.

On the first day of a lectureship I gave recently at Oxford University, the Oxford newspaper carried the story of the suicide of the student body president of an area college. After my lecture at the town hall that morning, I cannot begin to tell you the number of students who came to me to say that suicide is something they have toyed with.

In my travels across the globe, I have found this scenario to be conspicuous among our youth in universities everywhere as these institutions deliver meaninglessness in large doses. On campus after campus, in culture after culture, I have listened for hours to intellectuals, young and old, who testify to a deep-seated emptiness. Young, honest minds seek answers and meaning. No amount of philosophizing about a world without God brings hope. After three decades of covering every continent and delivering scores of university lectures, I have seen that this sense of alienation and meaninglessness is the principal malady of young minds. Academic degree after degree has not removed the haunting specter of the pointlessness of existence in a random universe. This deep malady of the soul will not be cured by writings such as Harris's. The momentary euphoria that may initially accompany a proclamation of liberation soon fades, and one finds oneself in the vise-like grip of despair in a life without ultimate purpose. A naturalistic framework offers no remedy for the sense of suffocation that ensues.

I am writing *The End of Reason* to tell young men and women—all who ask the hard questions about the meaning of life—that atheism is bankrupt for answers. The emperor has no clothes, and through his verbal magic Harris is trying hard to cover him up.

It may seem odd that I'm writing a letter to you in response to a man whose letter you may or may not have read. You may not wish to waste your time reading his book, but this response is intended to expose the systemic contradictions of his worldview and his cursory knowledge of other religions, which he has wielded with dangerous self-confidence. His book, like many books in America, has succeeded more because of its controversial nature than because of any real substance.

I also want to try to bridge the huge chasm that separates hostile atheists from those of us who believe in the Christ of the Scriptures and in the provision made in our Constitution and culture for those who wish to investigate the claims of any major religion and evaluate its truth or falsehood. The truth is, Harris's view rejects the very worldview that shaped the United States of America. His is a mind-set that, if it had been dominant at the time of America's emergence, would have never allowed for the formation of this nation. Thankfully, the America that *was* founded affirmed, implicitly or explicitly, our worldview while also allowing room for his. His America would ban our belief, leaving room only for the sovereignty of his materialistic or matter-driven vision of all human existence. Such is the demagoguery of his strident atheism.

With that said, let me get on with my letter to you. I begin my response to Harris with a humorous story, because I am quite sure the intensity of the text will increase as the letter unfolds.

THE
END
OF
REA
SON

Dear fellow American,

Two Australian sailors staggered out of a London pub into a dense fog and looked around for help. As they steadied themselves, they saw a man coming into the pub but evidently missed the military medals flashing on his dress uniform. One sailor blurted out, "Say, bloke, do you know where we are?" The officer, thoroughly offended, snarled in response, "Do you men know who I am?" The sailors looked at each other, and one said to the other, "We're really in a mess now. We don't know where we are, and he don't know who he is."

This story is appropriate to the discussion because, by the end of Sam Harris's *Letter to a Christian Nation*, we don't know who we are in essence or where we are in the grand scheme of a world without God. Harris's mass of verbiage has all the hallmarks of outdated, overused arguments (of the "weak point, shout louder" type) that are further weakened by a tragic misuse of the Bible and misunderstanding of Christianity and of other religions as well. But even as he rails against God, denying us any transcendent point of reference, he fully embraces God's life-defining prerogatives. His criticisms are caustic, his alternatives bankrupt. One of my professors at graduate school used to say of a critic, "He's better at smelling rotten eggs than at laying good ones." The eggs that Harris claims are rotten are, in fact, *good* eggs, while the eggs he has laid, claiming they are good, are the rotten ones.

As I read Sam Harris's books, *The End of Faith* and *Letter to a Christian Nation*, I felt as though I was being dragged through a vortex of emotion—from incredulity to outrage to a deep sadness. I wondered if anything was too sacred for him to mock. I bristled against the unvarnished disrespect, distortion, and illogicality of his thoughts that combined to reject any belief in God. It created a titanic struggle within me for an obvious reason: he has attacked that which lies at the very heart of my being and, need I say, of millions of others as well. His is a "take no prisoners" style—both fists flailing in an attempt to hit every conceivable expression of religion, Christianity in particular.

There is an English proverb that when you throw mud at others, you not only get your hands dirty but also lose a lot of ground. Harris may well have done that with his book. If he thinks his belief is noble, he has used ignoble and slanderous rhetoric to communicate it. Why his ridicule? Why such unbridled mockery? I fail to understand his extremist thinking, which has even caused other atheists embarrassment.

Atheists Divided on This New Atheism

Commenting on Richard Dawkins's book *The God Delusion*, which strikes many of the same notes as Harris's books, fellow atheist Michael Ruse, professor of philosophy at Florida State University, says, "*The God Delusion* makes me embarrassed to be an atheist." And in response to Sam Harris's presentation at the Salk Institute, atheist and professor of psychology Scott Atran used almost identical words: "I find it fascinating that among the brilliant scientists and philosophers at the conference, there was no convincing evidence presented that they know how to deal with the basic irrationality of human life other than to insist against all reason and evidence that things ought to be rational and evidence based. It makes me embarrassed to be a scientist and atheist."

Ruse and Atran restore my confidence in the sciences—unlike Harris and Dawkins, who make me leery of trusting in their findings when their prejudice is so venomous and obvious. Even with all the restraint I can muster, this is the most strongly worded book I have ever written, because I am alarmed at the cultural devastation wreaked by this kind of thinking.

Who Am I to Write This Response?

For those who do not know me, it may be helpful to introduce myself before I go any further. It may seem ironic that I, who hail from the East, now find myself pleading with a Westerner to remember where he has come from.

I was born to Indian parents and raised in India. My ancestors were priests from the highest caste of Hinduism in India's deep south. Religion is embedded in that culture, and India has probably spawned more religions than any other nation on earth. Hinduism alone boasts 330 million gods in its pantheon. Consequently, a lifetime of watching ceremony, ritual, superstition, and all that goes along with that worldview made me totally reject all belief in the supernatural. Many, many times I wondered how people could actually believe what they said they did, and I marveled at the masses' apparent commitment to gullibility. On this I agree with Sam Harris.

But never once did I consider the vitriol that Harris, Dawkins, and the new breed of atheists have spouted in their books and arguments. Frankly, rather than being so cavalier about their attitude, they would do better to seriously rethink whether they can accomplish what they are setting out to do by defacing the better part of humanity, among whom are Nobel laureates, brilliant philosophers and scientists, and others—peaceable men and women who have labored hard to make this a better world.

Now I readily admit that the accomplishments of these people did not justify their beliefs for me, but they did merit common courtesy and respect. Is it possible, however, that Harris's disrespect is justified because in an atheistic world, love for one's fellow human beings is a foreign concept? I certainly hope not. I know he tries to protect himself by tossing a bone now and then, saying, "I did qualify my position," but that's an old philosophical trick that is readily seen through. His impassioned hostility comes through loud and clear. There is nothing fragrant about atheism when its attitude smells like this.

My Exposure to the World's Religions

People often say that India is the most religious country in the world. It may be true, yet many in India live as practical atheists.

I was one of them.

I found religion to be an utter bore. Listening to priests—whether Hindu, Buddhist, Christian, or other—chanting what seemed to me to be inanities made me long to escape their so-called hallowed buildings. I saw their beliefs as superstition and fear-mongering, a means of boosting the egos of the perpetrators and controlling their followers, for a mantra repeated often enough eventually becomes indispensable to existence. Modern-day "guruism," especially of what I call the export variety, thrives in India today because the secularism exemplified in Europe and exported to the world leaves the inner person bankrupt and vulnerable to all kinds of beliefs. In Nietzschean terms, to me God was a manufactured entity. That was it, plain and simple.

But eventually, belief in a world birthed by accident, a life that has no purpose, morality without a point of reference except for those absolutes that have been smuggled in—well hidden behind the mask of relativism—and death that ends in oblivion made me prefer the possibility of this oblivion to the sheer weight of the emptiness of a God-less world. Contrary to what atheists imply, the dead weight of their beliefs leads to a heartless, pointless, and hollow existence. You may remember how the philosopher Friedrich Nietzsche, one of Sam Harris's predecessors in the promotion of atheism over belief in God, described existence without God. In such a world, Nietzsche said, we stray through an infinite nothing, with no up or down left. Lanterns must be lit in the morning hours and sacred games invented to take the place of religious ceremony. Finally, he said, a universal madness would break out when the truth of what mankind had done in killing God dawned on us. Nietzsche himself spent the last thirteen years of his life in the darkness of insanity, while his godly mother watched over him by his bedside.

Atheism Led to My Suicide Attempt

Albert Camus begins his essay "The Myth of Sisyphus" with these words: "There is only one really serious philosophical question, and that is suicide. Judging whether life is or is not worth living amounts to answering the fundamental question of philosophy." It is a haunting question; in fact, as I followed atheism to its logical conclusion in my own life as I grew up, it became my question.

Tragically, two of my close friends at college had already succeeded in their suicide attempts — one the heir to a highly successful business, the other a person who acted out of sheer aimlessness. Then it was my turn — a botched attempt in which I ended up in a hospital room in New Delhi, with doctors battling to keep me alive. It was in that lowly condition that I was handed a Bible, and the story of the gospel was read to me. All I can say now is how grateful I am that Sam Harris was not my mentor or his tirade my inspiration, for my life would have ended there and then. Instead, I trusted the Christ of the Scriptures, and today, four decades later, having traveled this globe dozens of times, speaking in numerous countries and lecturing in scores of universities, I find Jesus to be more beautiful and attractive than ever before.

This means absolutely nothing to the new atheists. But to me, to my family, and, I dare say, to tens of thousands of others in whose lives God has given me a small share, it has spelled the difference between despair and hope. This Jesus, whom I encountered in a moment of experience, I have tested through years of study and of seeking understanding. His description of the nature of reality and of everything within my own heart conforms to every test for truth to which I have submitted the teaching. I am as sure of my experience with him as I am of my own existence. It is little wonder that the common people of Jesus' day heard him gladly, and that when those marginalized by society were brought to him for judgment, he spoke words of comfort and indicted their accusers.

My Study of Atheism

For many years I have studied, researched, and written about the world's religions. But just to be fair to atheism, I walked the extra mile. As a visiting scholar at Cambridge University, I studied under a minister-turned-atheist, Don Cupitt, who was then dean of one of the colleges. Ironically, as an ordained Anglican priest, he was better known for his denial of God than for his service to God. I chose to study under him because I wanted to understand the case for atheism from a valid source. I wanted to hear and understand the full share of the argument for atheism once more, in case I had missed anything when I was younger.

Listening to this iconoclast, who, I dare say, would have cheered Sam Harris on, strained credulity. I found more heat than light in his arguments, more outrage than sensitivity to truth. His selective use of other religions was appalling, and when I dared to question him about what he was saying, his anger betrayed his lack of knowledge. Even those in the class who were themselves atheists chafed under his onslaught, feeling somewhat embarrassed. I realized then and there that what I had heard a seminary classmate say years ago was half true. When I asked this person who claimed to be an atheist why, if he were truly an unbeliever, he was studying in a school of divinity, he paused, popped open his Coke can, took a sip, leaned forward, and with a twinkle in his eye said, "There are big bucks in the God racket." Startled, I had to step back and take a deep breath. But I did have to give him full marks for being an honest charlatan. Now, after reading the likes of Sam Harris, Richard Dawkins, Christopher Hitchens, and Daniel Dennett in their anti-theistic outbursts, I have concluded that there are big bucks in the atheist racket as well.

I shall, however, grant them some benefit of the doubt with regard to their motives because, in their defense, an atheist who makes money by attacking the sacred is at least not pretending to be something else. And consistent with the atheistic worldview, their motives don't even need much justification, since in a world without absolutes any motive will do—and no motive is even necessary.

We All Start from Paradigms

Where do I begin to unpack the systemic contradictions between the atheistic worldview Sam Harris espouses and the assumptions he makes? Perhaps the best starting point would be to tell you why I am not an atheist. As you well know, everyone has a worldview. A worldview basically offers answers to four necessary questions—questions that relate to origin, meaning, morality, and hope that assures a destiny. These answers must be correspondingly true and, as a whole, coherent.

Origin

Let me start with origin, for it is here that Sam Harris takes his first shot. I will save a fuller scientific and philosophical discussion for later. Right now, I simply wish to differentiate between God and accident. How did life come to be?

Big Bang cosmology, along with Einstein's theory of general relativity, implies that there is indeed an "in the beginning."* All the data indicates a universe that is exploding outward from a point of infinite density. We know quite well that this singularity is not really a point; it is the whole of three-dimensional space compressed to zero size. This, in fact, actually represents a boundary at which space

_____

* Unless, of course, Harris wants to philosophize, as theoretical physicist Stephen Hawking does, about a universe without boundary or edge and go the route of a "world ensemble cosmology" and imaginary time. John Polkinghorne, professor of mathematical physics at Queens College, Cambridge, a colleague of Hawking, had just one response to that proposition for those of us studying under him: "Let's recognize imagination for what it is." (The quote is from my class notes, but I found a similar statement in his book *One World: The Interaction of Science and Theology* [London: SPCK, 1986], 80: "Let us recognize these speculations for what they are. They are not physics but, in the strictest sense, metaphysics.") Hawking does grant a "beginning." He just lacks a beginning point. In his extensions, Hawking is simply engaging in bad metaphysics.

ceases to exist. Even the terms plead for explanation. The point I wish to make here (if you'll pardon the pun) is that at the point of the universe's origin, there is *something* rather than *nothing*—a mystery that leaves science totally silent.

Nothing *Cannot Produce* Something

Not only is there something; the laws of science actually break down right at the beginning. The very starting point for an atheistic universe is based on something that cannot explain its own existence. The scientific laws by which atheists want all certainty established do not even exist as a category at the beginning of the universe because, according to those laws of science by which atheists want to measure all things, matter cannot simply "pop into existence" on its own.

The silence from atheistic science on why there is something rather than nothing is deafening. Atheistic philosopher Bertrand Russell said that the universe is "just there." But that clearly is not a scientific explanation. According to science, nothing that exists (or that is) can explain its own existence. Yet, according to their cosmology, we just happen to be. This means that any *purpose* for our being is as random as any *cause* for our being. Atheist Stephen Jay Gould makes this observation:

> We are here because one odd group of fishes had a peculiar fin anatomy that could transform

into legs for terrestrial creatures; because comets struck the earth and wiped out dinosaurs, thereby giving mammals a chance not otherwise available (so thank your lucky stars in a literal sense); because the earth never froze entirely during an ice age; because a small and tenuous species, arising in Africa a quarter of a million years ago, has managed, so far, to survive by hook and by crook. We may yearn for a "higher" answer—but none exists.... We cannot read the meaning of life passively in the facts of nature. We must construct these answers ourselves—from our own wisdom and ethical sense. There is no other way.

How do you like that? At one point in his argument Gould makes the astounding comment that once you latch on to the truthfulness of this reality —that there is no reality other than the one we make for ourselves—far from being disheartening, it is quite liberating. Well, I'm glad *he* felt liberated, because millions of others do not feel liberated when life becomes a question mark.

But notice where Gould is silent. He credits astral collisions for making it possible for mankind to inhabit planet Earth by destroying already existing life-forms, but where did these stars and comets and planets come from? Doesn't it worry him that his own paradigm is silent on the question of origins? The best we can get from people such as

Gould and Harris is that, yes, we know it's a problem and one day we'll have the answer to it.

As we know it now, all order did not evolve. Nothing in science supports this contention. Something had to exist as an explanation in itself. Nothing does not produce something—and never has.

The Odds of Random Life

The vacuousness of the atheistic approach to the universe's origin is illustrated by Nobel laureate and atheist Francis Crick's* answer to the question of how life around us began: "Probably because a spaceship from another planet brought spores to seed the earth." Carl Sagan went to his grave "viewing the whole universe as nothing more than molecules in motion." He believed that some extraterrestrial entity would be able to explain us to ourselves and thereby justified the billions of dollars spent on listening in on outer space, watching and waiting for some contact.

I hate to admit it, but there is actually a minister in a city in America who has a phone line connected from his wife's grave to his office because before she died, they had agreed that if she was privy to any inside word that Jesus' second coming was imminent, she would call him so that he would be the first to know. This man is to the Christian

---

* Francis Crick is the codiscoverer of the structure of the DNA molecule.

world what those who talk about spaceships are to the atheist world—promoting a phantom idea, a worldview based on nothing but mystification and speculation.

Let me take this a little further. Donald Page of Princeton's Institute for Advanced Science has calculated the odds against our universe randomly taking a form suitable for life as one out of $10,000,000,000^{124}$—a number that exceeds all imagination. Astronomers Fred Hoyle and N. C. Wickramasinghe found that the odds of the random formation of a single enzyme from amino acids anywhere on our planet's surface are one in 10^{20}. Furthermore, they observe, "The trouble is that there are about two thousand enzymes and the chance of obtaining them all in a random trial is only one part in $(10^{20})^{20,000} = 10^{40,000}$, an outrageously small probability that could not be faced even if the whole universe consisted of organic soup." And this is just one step in the formation of life. Nothing has yet been said about DNA and where it came from, or of the transcription of DNA to RNA, which scientists admit cannot even be numerically computed. Nor has anything been said of mitosis or meiosis. One would have to conclude that the chance of the random ordering of organic molecules is not essentially different from a big fat zero. Perhaps that's why they call it a singularity, because it is without definition or empirical explanation.

That's the zero to which Sam Harris gives credit for everything; that's his explanation for why we are here. And if one accepts this explanation, the resulting pointlessness of existence is devastating to our hunger for significance. It is little wonder that this belief hasn't taken root with billions of people, who will still seek God, no matter how loudly Harris protests. The cry of reason is irrepressible, and the average person can see through the illogicality of the claims of atheism and the emptiness they lead to. I know all the responses, the arguments declaring that in spite of all the statistical improbabilities we are still here and this proves we have come from such origins. I know this is enough reason for the skeptic. But the assumptions and deductions they have to make leave us marveling that people who say they believe these things actually do believe them—deductions, I might add, that you would never make from microprocesses in the lab or in daily living or in the courtroom. In his search for extraterrestrial intelligence, Carl Sagan said all we need is one message with information in it from outer space and we'd be able to recognize the presence of intelligence. We won't even need to translate the message, he said; we'll just recognize the presence of intelligence. When it suits the atheist, only intelligence can explain intelligibility, but when it is discomforting, primordial self-existent soup will do. They cannot hide their prejudices.

Is it any wonder that Antony Flew, who carried the atheistic flag for decades, now begs off atheism because it simply cannot explain this intelligibility?

Belief in a Creator Does Not Hinge on How He Created

I want to add that our arguments for the existence of God do not hinge on debunking evolution. Evolution is a straw man that has been thrown up, as if all that needs to be done to achieve the crashing down of belief in God is to posit evolution. Serious intellectuals ought to know that no worldview is established on one knockout argument. Later in this letter I will investigate in more detail specific arguments for Christian theism. For now, all I want to assert is that the atheistic starting point brings us to a contradiction in terms at worst and a random universe at best. In *Miracles*, C. S. Lewis takes this kind of thinking to task: "Reason might conceivably be found to depend on [another reason] and so on; it would not matter how far this process was carried provided you found Reason coming from Reason at each stage. It is only when you are asked to believe in Reason coming from non-reason that you must cry Halt."

I read what Sam Harris has written and cry halt. Can he really posit a transcendent basis for reasoning when his original source is not reason itself? He is locked into the stranglehold of material determinism, where what you end up with is predetermined by what you start out with. If non-moral, non-reasoning matter is all there was in the beginning, the result can only be what non-moral, non-reasoning matter produces. Every succeeding stage will be predetermined to be without moral or intentional significance. In fact, Richard Dawkins says in his theory of "memes" that this is how religion has been perpetrated, predetermined by birth and ancestry.*

Isn't it interesting that such determinism is the curse and the cause of religious belief but atheists are able to break outside the box of determinism and think for themselves? Apparently they are not bound by the same restrictions that bind the rest of us. After years in the academy I have learned a trade secret: If you know enough about a subject, you can confuse anybody by a selective use of the facts. The inescapable fact for the atheist is that life is the random product of time plus matter plus chance.

---

* Richard Dawkins first introduced the term *memes* in his book *The Selfish Gene* (Oxford: Oxford Univ. Press, 1976). He argues that religion is a "mental virus of faith" in his essay "Viruses of the Mind," *Free Inquiry* (Summer 1993), 34–41.

Meaning

If life is random, then the inescapable consequence, first and foremost, is that there can be no ultimate meaning and purpose to existence. This consequence is the existential Achilles' heel of atheistic belief. As individuals and collectively as cultures, we humans long for meaning. But if life is random, we have climbed the evolutionary ladder only to find nothing at the top.

This is another theme on which Sam Harris's alternative answers are hollow. He seems to harp on how God acts like such a criminal and how we live such precarious lives that even one tragedy should shatter our tranquillity. The experience of pain in this world proves to him the meaninglessness of life.

Pleasure—Not Pain—Is the Death Knell of Meaning

The famed twentieth-century British journalist Malcolm Muggeridge once said that all news is old things happening to new people. From the naturalist Scottish philosopher David Hume to the existentialist Jean-Paul Sartre, the list of grievances resulting from the problem of pain in the world has been stated over and over. I suggest they have missed the point.

Author and satirist G. K. Chesterton remarked that meaninglessness does not come from being weary of pain but from being weary of pleasure.

Pleasure, not pain, is the death knell of meaning. This is the lonely planet problem of Sam Harris's worldview—the belief that because each of us is alone in the universe our personal joys and sorrows have no effect or impact on anyone else. In other words, it's all about me. We have all come to know that our problem is not that pain has produced emptiness in our lives; the real problem is that even pleasure ultimately leaves us empty and unfulfilled. When the pleasure button is pressed incessantly, we are left feeling bewilderingly empty and betrayed.

When I read the biography of Oscar Wilde and researched the life of this quintessential hedonist, I was repeatedly surprised by the protracted passages of despair that came from the heart and the pen of a man so completely devoted to the pursuit of pleasure. See the Scripture reference—Job 29:22—engraved in Latin on his tombstone, which translates as, "After I had spoken, they spoke no more; my words fell gently on their ears." Ponder the epitaph there that reads, "And alien tears will fill for him pity's long-broken urn, for his mourners will be outcast men, and outcasts always mourn."* These speak of the silence of pain. If it were pain alone that brought emptiness, I would at least half grant the atheist's point. But some of the loneli-

---

* The words of the epitaph come from Oscar Wilde's poem "The Ballad of Reading Gaol."

est people I have met or read about are those who have had everything and experienced little of what we usually consider pain; yet, they too have pain—pain resulting from having indulged and come away empty.

The greatest disappointment (and resulting pain) you can feel is when you have just experienced that which you thought would bring you the ultimate in pleasure—and it has let you down. Pleasure without boundaries produces a life without purpose. That is real pain. No death, no tragedy, no atrocity—*nothing* really matters. Life is sheer hollowness, with no purpose.

In Atheism There Are No Ultimate Answers

A while ago, a man left a suicide note in Las Vegas, the city of glitz and gambling. The note summarized his despair this way: *Here there are no answers.* This is the inescapable conclusion of Sam Harris's book, no matter how hard he tries to cosmetically dress up his worldview, because his worldview is bankrupt. He may try to convince us otherwise, but underneath the arguments it's all bad news: we are all there is, alone in this world.

Sam Harris isn't the first to mount an attack against religious belief; nor will he be the last, I'm sure. Religion suffered a mortal wound in Europe when the ecclesiastical powers joined hands with the oppressing political powers (many of whom were atheists) and tightened the screws on the masses—France has never recovered from its experience. But philosophers such as Voltaire, who theorized on the fallacies of religion, had no better answer to give to the masses they had rescued from what they considered religious "tyranny." Here is what Voltaire wrote:

I am a puny part of the great whole.
Yes; but all animals condemned to live,
All sentient things, born by the same stern law,
Suffer like me, and like me also die.
The vulture fastens on his timid prey,
And stabs with bloody beak the quivering limbs:
All's well, it seems, for it. But in a while
An eagle tears the vulture into shreds;
The eagle is transfixed by shaft of man;
The man, prone in the dust of battlefield,
Mingling his blood with dying fellow-men,
Becomes in turn the food of ravenous birds.

Thus the whole world in every member groans:
All born for torment and for mutual death.
And o'er this ghastly chaos you would say
The ills of each make up the good of all!
What blessedness! And as, with quaking voice,
Mortal and pitiful, ye cry, "All's well,"
The universe belies you, and your heart
Refutes a hundred times your mind's conceit....

What is the verdict of the vastest mind?
Silence: the book of fate is closed to us.

Man is a stranger to his own research;
He knows not whence he comes, nor whither goes.
Tormented atoms in a bed of mud,
Devoured by death, a mockery of fate.

Voltaire is reported to have said that within a hundred years of his day the Bible would be a forgotten book. In a strange twist of irony, within a century of his death, one of his homes in France would belong to the Geneva Bible Society and serve as the place where Bibles were printed and distributed. But at least Voltaire, Sartre, and Nietzsche were honest and consistent in their views. They admitted the ridiculousness of life, the pointlessness of everything in an atheistic world. Contemporary atheists such as Richard Dawkins and Sam Harris, however, are so blind to the conceit of their own minds that they try to present this view of life as some sort of triumphal liberation. Sartre, as atheistic intellectual elites know but are embarrassed to acknowledge, denounced atheism on his deathbed as philosophically unlivable.* A few years ago, in a

---

* See Thomas Molnar, "Jean–Paul Sartre, RIP: A Late Return," *National Review* 34 (June 11, 1982): 677: "It is sufficient to quote a single sentence from what Sartre said then to measure the degree of his acceptance of the grace of God and the creatureliness of man: 'I do not feel that I am the product of chance, a speck of dust in the universe, but someone who was expected, prepared, prefigured. In short, a being whom only a Creator could put here; and this idea of a creating hand refers to God.'" Quoted in Josh McDowell and Don Stewart, "Existentialism," *http://www.greatcom.org/resources/secular_religions/ch04/default.htm* (accessed October 1, 2007).

debate between atheism and Christianity, Antony Flew described a Christian philosopher's experience of knowing Christ as "grotesque." But Flew has now vacated the atheistic camp, no longer able to honestly justify its metaphysical moorings. For all practical purposes, Flew is now a Deist, one who believes in God, albeit seeing him as a distant god who takes no active part in the lives of men and women.

Atheism Taken to Its Logical Conclusions

Probably the best example of atheism's working out to its logical conclusions in the life of a human being is Michel Foucault. In the spring of 1975 he sat at the edge of a cliff. With two young Americans beside him and the music of Karlheinz Stockhausen's *Kontakte* in the background, he deliberately chose to lose contact with reality and give in to his imagination, induced by LSD. Lying back on the ground, he threw his hands in the air and cried, "The stars are raining down on me. The sky has exploded. I know this is not true. But it is the Truth." He carved his creed—"it is forbidden to forbid"—into the minds of his students. Sliding down the slippery slope of pleasure without fences to guide him or the encumbrance of moral conviction to slow his fall, he gradually associated even death with pleasure. "I would like and hope I'll die of an overdose of pleasure of any kind," he said. He gambled away his life in the game of lust he played:

"To die for the love of boys ... what could be more beautiful." His lifestyle of mindless abandon ended pitifully, dissolute to every cell of his being. Ravaged by AIDS, he self-destructed.

Foucault was one of the products of atheism, and he said many of the same things Sam Harris is saying. For Harris to deny that Foucault is a product of atheistic thinking would mean he would have to reconsider his appraisal of all forms of Christian expression with the same judgment. Harris just happens to borrow from a worldview better than his own while castigating it at the same time. Life without God is ultimately life without any point of reference for meaning other than what one gives it at the time.

Remember what the atheist Stephen Jay Gould said about meaning? "We may yearn for a 'higher' answer—but none exists." Now read Foucault's answers to a student:

STUDENT: Should I take chances with my life?
FOUCAULT: By all means! Take risks, go out on a limb!
STUDENT: But I yearn for solutions.
FOUCAULT: There are no solutions.
STUDENT: Then at least some answers.
FOUCAULT: There are no answers!

At least Foucault was honest about life's lack of meaning for those who reject God.

I think of the story of a woman who was a passenger on a plane suddenly caught in heavy turbulence. She panicked and nearly passed out. The copilot came to calm her down.

"Look out the right side of the plane," he said. "Do you see that light flashing at the end of the wingtip?"

"Yes, I do," she stammered.

"Now look out the left side of the aircraft. Do you see a light flashing at the end of that wingtip?"

"Yes, I do," she whispered.

"As long as we stay between those two lights, we're safe," he said, which brought enormous comfort to the passenger.

That is atheism's only answer to the pursuit of meaning. It is a false comfort with self-referencing beacons. Two planes could be on a collision course if these two wingtips with blinking lights are all that is guiding them.

Morality

Not only does atheism's worldview lead to the death of meaning; it also leads to the death of moral reasoning.

For those who haven't read Sam Harris's *Letter to a Christian Nation*, let me lay out his argument on this point. Harris writes that if God does exist and takes an interest in the affairs of human beings, it should be easy to see what he's up to. The only thing that becomes puzzling to him then is that "so many otherwise rational men and women" deny the horror of the kind of events he describes and consider God to be acting according to the height of moral wisdom (*Letter*, 48).

The examples he cites with passionate and dramatic language designed to tug at your heartstrings include the rape, torture, and murder of "a little girl," which he says is happening as you are reading his letter — or if not at that exact moment, in a few hours or days. And he expresses his dismay that statistics suggest that the parents of such a little girl (as well as you, his reader) are likely to believe that an all-powerful and all-loving God is watching over them and their little girl even as this atrocity is taking place. Harris asks whether it is right or good that you — and they — should believe in this God (*Letter*, 50–51).

His short answer to his own question is a categorical and emphatic *no*. And that, he says, is atheism. Rather than a philosophy or a worldview, Harris says atheism is simply a refusal to deny what a person should see as obvious — that there is no God (because this is obvious to Harris). Therefore he insists that the term "atheism" shouldn't exist, just as "no one needs to identify himself as a 'non-astrologer' or a 'non-alchemist'" (*Letter*, 51).

Examples of what Harris sees as God's failure to protect humanity are to be seen everywhere, he says, such as the massive destruction in the city of New Orleans brought about by a hurricane in 2005. What was God doing while Katrina laid waste to New Orleans, he asks? Didn't he hear the prayers of those who "fled the rising waters for the safety of their attics, only to be slowly drowned there"? These people, Harris insists, "died talking to an imaginary friend" (*Letter*, 52).

Harris states adamantly and unconditionally that it is disgraceful for survivors of a catastrophe of any kind to believe that a loving God has spared them while allowing others to die, including "infants in their cribs" (*Letter*, 54). (You see how he continually appeals to your emotions!) And then he claims that only after you, the reader, have ceased to excuse or try to explain the suffering in the world by using "religious fantasies" will you truly understand just how precious life is and how unfortunate it is that suffering takes place at all, as there is really no reason for suffering other than to interfere with someone's pursuit of happiness (*Letter*, 54).

This is supposedly his linchpin argument, but it's given with his feet firmly planted in midair. There is so much philosophical hollowness here that I wonder where to begin in responding to what he says. Once again, we see the old evidential argument of evil against God's existence, which ends up moralizing while building its entire edifice on matter. I am reminded of the old Irish farmer who was asked for directions by a tourist who had lost his way. "If that's where you want to go," said the farmer, "this is not where I would begin."

Should Atheists Be Classified as Such?

Sam Harris does not believe that atheism should be a philosophical category. He notes that one does not describe himself or herself as a "non-alchemist" or "non-astrologer" (*Letter*, 51). But if in a discussion about your future someone looks at your hand and asks for your date of birth so that he can study the planetary alignment that day, it might be to your advantage to know whether he is in fact an astrologer or a pizza maker who reads palms as an avocation. If you are facing serious health issues and a stranger gives you a potion to drink, it would be of interest to know whether this is an alchemist or a pharmacist or a witch doctor you are dealing with. When you are debating every definition of life ranging from origin to destiny, it makes sense to know whether you hold to an atheistic worldview or to something else.

But this is not atypical. Existentialists did not want to be classified; postmodernists do not want to be boxed in. They just want to be able to stigmatize others without attaching a name to themselves. They shun categorization of anything to which they hold (though they comfortably categorize others, including God). The reason is this: *it does not hold.* They look for a universal solvent to dissolve the notion of God. With predictable result, they end up only dissolving their own worldview.

I find it interesting that this group of people who don't want to be categorized held a September 2007 conference at which Sam Harris was one of the speakers—and the conference theme was "Crystal Clear Atheism." If Harris and others do not believe that atheism should be a philosophical category, the choice of the theme is puzzling.

Does the Reality of Evil Mean There Is No God?

When Sam Harris asks what God was doing when Hurricane Katrina destroyed New Orleans (*Letter,* 52) and why God does not prevent the rape, torture, and murder of children (*Letter,* 51), what is he *really* saying? Is he saying that such things are evil, ought to be evil, or ought not to be allowed by a loving God? In any of the three assertions he is at best saying, "I do not see a moral order at work here." But if there is no God, who has the authority to say whether there is a moral order in operation? Sam Harris? Adolf Hitler? *Who?*

In addition to hitting God for hurricanes, rape, torture, and murder, Harris lays the Holocaust at the door of medieval Christianity. Harris's view is basically that the anti-Semitism spawned by Christians during medieval times led to the Holocaust at the hands of the Nazis (*Letter*, 41–42).

But why does Harris stop with medieval times? Why not go further into history? This argument has as much merit as Iran's President Mahmoud Ahmadinejad arguing that the Holocaust never happened. For one who doesn't believe there was an initial cause to the universe, Harris is certainly quick to identify what he considers the causes for certain wrongdoing.

Has Harris read about Hitler's own spiritual journey? Has he read anything about Hitler's dabbling in the occult? Is he aware that Hitler personally presented the writings of Nietzsche to Stalin and Mussolini? Is he ignoring the fact that others who were not Jewish were also slaughtered by Hitler? Did he read Nazi mastermind Adolf Eichmann's last words that refused repentance and denied belief in God? Does he know how many Russians were killed by the Nazi machine? Does he recall Hitler's words inscribed over one of the gas ovens in Auschwitz—"I want to raise a generation of young people devoid of a conscience, imperious, relentless and cruel"? Does he know that Hitler's point was that the destruction of the weak is a good thing for the survival of the strong and that "nature intended it that way," as is taught by atheistic evolution's tenet of natural selection (described by Voltaire in the poem I have already cited)—"the survival of the fittest"? None of these signs of the Holocaust point back to Christianity.

For Harris to convince us that Hitler was wrong to do what he did, he has to borrow from an objective moral framework to support his point. Let me put it another way. If Harris's assertion that no moral order is visible in the world is true, we may well ask why Hitler couldn't introduce his own order. What was wrong with what he did? What is the basis on which Harris is calling Hitler immoral? Or is he calling him immoral?

How conveniently the atheist plays word games! When it is Stalin or Pol Pot who does the slaughtering, it is because they are deranged or irrational ideologues; their atheism has nothing to do with their actions. But when a Holocaust is engendered by an ideologue, it is the culmination of four hundred years of Christian intolerance for the Jew. Has it occurred to Sam Harris that his book might sow the seeds for the slaughter of Christians? Has he paused to think of what motivates him to write these things against a group of people? What would he say if two hundred years from now someone says that genocide against Christians can be traced back to the anti-Christian writings of Sam Harris?

Atheists can't have it both ways. If the murder of innocents is wrong, it is wrong not because science tells us it is wrong but because every life has intrinsic worth—a postulate that atheism simply cannot deduce. There is no way for Harris as an atheist to argue for moral preferences except by his own subjective means, that is, his personal preference or environment. One cannot make absolute statements based on one's personal feelings on a matter. That fact provides the very reason his own genre of writers within naturalism's frame of reference* admit that moral reasoning is not rational apart from God. Their philosophical word games are nothing more than an attempt to escape the stifling unreason to which they are driven.

What is the objective moral framework Harris adopts on which he has built his entire critique of God? His emotion-laden critique hangs on an argument that says, "I can see no moral framework operating in the world, but what I do see is morally condemnable." In philosophical terms, this is called a mutually exclusive assumption. Therefore, the moral framework he is forced to adopt is, in reality, one he built himself.

Given this, it is little wonder that Bertrand Russell admitted he couldn't live as though ethical values were simply a matter of personal taste and that he therefore found his own views "incredible." "I do not know the solution," he said. In an earlier debate

---

* Naturalism's assumption is that nature is all we have.

with Jesuit priest Frederick Copleston, Russell had tried another route to get around objective morality and ended up looking bad. When Copleston asked him how he differentiated between good and bad, Russell answered, "I don't have any justification any more than I have when I distinguish between blue and yellow.... I can see they are different."

"Well, that is an excellent justification, I agree," said Copleston. "You distinguish blue and yellow by seeing them, so you distinguish good and bad by what faculty?"

"By my feelings," was Russell's reply.

Father Copleston was kind. The next question was staring Russell in the face but wasn't asked because he already looked so weak in that part of the discussion. The question that should have been asked was, "Mr. Russell, in some cultures they love their neighbors; in other cultures they eat them. Do you have a personal preference, and if so, what is it?"

Russell's agnosticism and ambiguity about his own views on ethical values were at least more honest than Harris's morality concocted in his own mind—as if morality should be self-evident to everybody, regardless of whether God exists or not. Harris's antagonism toward God ends up proving that he intuitively finds some things reprehensible. But he cannot explain his innate sense of right and wrong—the reality of God's law written on his heart—because there is no logical explanation for how that intuition toward morality could develop from sheer matter and chemistry.

Popularly stated, I would put it in this way:

- When you assert that there is such a thing as evil, you must assume there is such a thing as good.
- When you say there is such a thing as good, you must assume there is a moral law by which to distinguish between good and evil. There must be some standard by which to determine what is good and what is evil.
- When you assume a moral law, you must posit a moral lawgiver—the source of the moral law.

But this moral lawgiver is precisely who atheists are trying to disprove.

Can Morality Exist Apart from a Moral Lawgiver?

Sam Harris may protest, "Why is a moral lawgiver necessary in order to recognize good and evil?" For the simple reason that a moral affirmation cannot remain an abstraction. The person who moralizes assumes intrinsic worth in himself or herself and transfers intrinsic worth to the life of another, and thus he or she considers that life worthy of protection (as in the illustrations Harris gives, namely, rape, torture, murder, and natural catastrophes). Transcending value must come from a person of transcending worth. But in a world in which matter alone exists there can be no intrinsic worth. Let me put it in philosophical terms:

- Objective moral values exist only if God exists.
- Objective moral values do exist [a point Harris concedes in his letter].
- Therefore God exists.

An examination of these premises and their validity presents a very strong argument for the existence of God. In fact, J. L. Mackie, a vociferous atheist who challenged the existence of God on the basis of the reality of evil, granted at least this logical connection when he said, "We might well argue ... that objective, intrinsically prescriptive features, supervenient upon natural ones, constitute so odd a cluster of qualities and relations that they are most unlikely to have arisen in the ordinary course of events, without an all-powerful God to create them."

Therefore, we must agree with the conclusion that *nothing can be intrinsically prescriptively good unless there also exists a God who has fashioned the universe thus*. But this is the very Being Harris denies exists because of the existence of evil.

Can Reason Alone Provide
a Moral Framework?

Positing a world devoid of a moral framework, Harris opts for "reason" as the source for his unbelief in God while maintaining belief in a moral code. But listen, then, to the words of Canadian philosopher Kai Nielsen, who is prolific in his writings in defense of atheism: "Reason doesn't decide here. The picture I have painted for you is not a pleasant one. Reflection on it depresses me. Pure practical reason, even with a good knowledge of the facts, will not take you to morality."

So on his own terms as an atheist, Sam Harris is either engaging in moral reasoning that is only valid if God exists, or he is being irrational in his assertions.

It still remains for him to say that God breaks his own laws and is therefore evil or contradictory. But by doing so, he would be claiming an innate ability to recognize the violation of one's own moral law as a moral failure.

Harris is clearly assuming that God kills innocent people (see *Letter*, 52–54), and thus he is violating his own laws. Let's grant this for a moment. Why is killing innocents wrong? Is it wrong because God says so? Is it wrong because Harris believes that an innocent ought not to be killed? If we assume the first, namely, it is wrong because God says it is wrong, then God contradicts himself through his actions—saying it is wrong but killing innocents anyway. Harris, however, is not relieved of the responsibility of proving his argument that innocents ought not to be killed. To genuinely believe this he must assume a moral framework that supports the intrinsic value of innocent life. But based on his atheistic starting point, he has no grounds for such a moral framework.

This leaves us with a third option—one that Harris has completely ignored or refused to consider: he is selectively borrowing from the biblical revelation of justice and retribution while ignoring the big story into which it fits and by which it gains its purpose. His moral argument distorts the Bible's finer points while denying its big picture.

Christianity teaches that every single life has ultimate value. In secularism, while there is no ultimate value to a life, the atheist subjectively selects particular values to applaud. This game is played every day by the relativist camp, while it refuses to allow the other side the benefit of playing by the same rules.

We Can't Have Free Will without Suffering

If Sam Harris wishes to talk about suffering, he must talk about human autonomy versus God's story of why we are the way we are. Though the sacred is offered to us, the will is arrogant and refuses to submit to God's authority. No one of us is any different from or better than any other; some just mask their true nature better. The story of suffering cannot be told without the story of human pride and of our need for God to change our hearts.

Is Harris really demanding that God create in us the ability to love without giving us the option to reject that love, the desire to trust and to be trusted without the freedom to doubt, the privilege of making a choice without the responsibility of accepting the ramifications of that choice? I find appalling his deft use of language to sweep the human predicament under the rug. He considers God, "if [he] exists," to be "the most prolific abortionist of all" (*Letter*, 38), saying that even one death at God's hands is unacceptable, while he himself looks the other way as millions of unborn children are aborted.

Whose Moral Right? Ours? Or God's?

Some years ago, the well-known astronomer Hugh Ross and I were taking part in a radio talk show at Ohio State University. We were discussing some theme related to the origin of the universe when an irate woman called in and began to attack us with a volley of words. Her charge was that our conversation was really nothing more than a smoke screen for reversing Roe versus Wade and taking away a woman's right to an abortion. Remember, we were talking about the origin of the universe.

Throughout her tirade she repeatedly insisted, "It's my moral right to do what I choose to do with my body!"

Finally, when she paused for a breath, I said, "All right ma'am, since you brought it up, I'd like to ask you a question. Can you explain something to me? When a plane crashes and some die while others live, a skeptic calls into question God's moral character, saying that he has chosen some to live and others to die on a whim; yet you say it is your moral right to choose whether the child within you should live or die. Does that not sound odd to you? When God decides who should live or die, he is immoral. When you decide who should live or die, it's your moral right."

There was a pin-drop silence.

A person may dismissively say that he or she does not see a moral order. But I strongly suspect that the real issue is not an absence of moral order in the world but the insistence on determining for oneself what is good and what is evil, in spite of what we intuitively know to be true. Let's be honest. To believe that there is no moral order, one must assume knowledge of what a moral order would look like if there were one. But why should one person's opinion of what the moral order should look like be any more authentic than anyone else's? And besides, if there truly is no moral order, any attempt to enforce one is sheer pragmatism, open to any challenge for other pragmatic reasons.

On the other hand, before the charge is made that the God of the Bible violates his own moral order, ought one not consider the fact that the same God who gave the moral law also gives the reasons he allows pain and suffering? Why debate, even for the sake of argument, the possibility that God has given a moral law and ignore the reasoning that accompanies it?

We Naturally Resist God's Moral Order

Why do we humans naturally resist God's moral order? Because behind all the arguments is a clenched fist, like that of former Russian premier Joseph Stalin, whose last gesture before he died was to raise himself up in his bed and shake his fist toward heaven. Sam Harris and Richard Dawkins are, in effect, doing the same thing while in the prime of their lives. Beneath all the intellectual verbiage is a covert desire to have a world without God. Why? Aldous Huxley answered on behalf of all skeptics when he wrote that he *wanted* the world not to have meaning so that he would be set free from all the moral demands of religion. Yet how ironic that, while he repudiated meaning, he decried the moral incapacity of science: "We are living now, not in the delicious intoxication induced by the early successes of science, but in a rather grisly morning-after, when it has become quite apparent that what triumphant science has done hitherto is to improve the means for achieving unimproved or actually deteriorated ends."

Fascinating, coming from Huxley, isn't it? The science he touts as the savior of the world has no moral impetus within it. But then, why should we be surprised? That is not science's role. Even Richard Dawkins, Harris's hero, admits that science has no methods or authority for deciding what is ethical. And scholars such as the Hungarian scientist Michael Polanyi have spent their lives as philosophers of science warning against this hegemony that atheists seek.

Though Viktor Frankl was an inmate in Auschwitz, he didn't blame God for the Holocaust. He laid the blame for that horror at the feet of men and women who thought like Sam Harris. Listen to Frankl's words in *The Doctor and the Soul*:

> If we present a man with a concept of man which is not true, we may well corrupt him. When we present man as an automaton of reflexes, as a mind-machine, as a bundle of instincts, as a pawn of drives and reactions, as a mere product of instinct, heredity, and environment, we feed the nihilism to which modern man is, in any case, prone.
>
> I became acquainted with the last stage of that corruption in my second concentration camp,

Auschwitz. The gas chambers of Auschwitz were the ultimate consequence of the theory that man is nothing but the product of heredity and environment—or, as the Nazi liked to say, "of Blood and Soil." I am absolutely convinced that the gas chambers of Auschwitz, Treblinka, and Maidanek were ultimately prepared not in some Ministry or other in Berlin, but rather at the desks and in the lecture halls of nihilistic scientists and philosophers.

In an interview with *The Wall Street Journal* in April 2007, Indonesia's former president, Abdurrahman Wahid, was very clear about where he lays the blame for Islamic fundamentalism. He himself is moderate and pro-West in his thinking, taking his life in his hands for being so. He specifically states that university students in his land are railing not against the democratic process but against the radical belief that scientific knowledge is the *only* knowledge—a belief that eradicates the soul. It is the enforced anti-God state of mind that is driving many into the hands of the other extreme. Isn't it ironic that when Islam is in a position of power, Islamic beliefs are forced on everyone, and that when atheism has the upper hand, atheistic beliefs are enforced on everyone? Only in Christianity is the privilege given both to believe and to disbelieve without any enforcement.

Are Atheists More "Moral" Than Others?

Sam Harris asks, "When was the last atheist riot?" (*Letter*, 39). Has he ever recognized the link between his system of thought and the violent radicals at the end of the spectrum? Ideas do have consequences. Thought is the precursor to action, and the incitement of his kind of inflammatory language may well spawn the very thing he is so magnanimously denying. Has he not seen the violence that takes place during trade union strikes in Europe? There were atheists present, you know. Has he not heard of the riots in the Watts neighborhood of Los Angeles and in other places? There were atheists present, you know. Has he not read of the extermination machine instituted by Stalin after he abandoned God and became an atheist?

Now let me ask you this: Did you see any rioting after the release of the movie based on Nikos Kazantzakis's novel *The Last Temptation of Christ*? Did you see any rioting after the exhibit of Andres Serrano's "artwork"—a photograph of a crucifix immersed in urine? Did you see any movie theaters burned down after the sophomoric *The DaVinci Code* was shown—or after the most recent farce in March 2007, when the Discovery Channel aired a documentary claiming that the bones of Jesus were found in a Jerusalem tomb in 1980? (I might add that if all of these stories were true, you would *have* to believe in the supernatural to have Mary Magdalene in so many places at the same time!)

I wonder what would happen if a movie that exposed homosexual practices, using medical research to evaluate the practice, were shown in our theaters. I wonder what would happen if the teaching of atheism were barred from our university campuses. We might see riots until now unparalleled.

Atheists do not need to riot. They have gradually taken away our right to even speak in the academy. They wish to silence us. When I was at Oxford recently, I was told about an article written by Richard Dawkins in which he advocated that any prospective student with a creationist point of view should be refused admittance into Oxford. And he criticizes the intolerance of religion? Dawkins is a professor at Oxford, a university whose motto is "The Lord Is My Light." He has been given privileges to teach because of the Judeo-Christian ethic of tolerance. And now that he is in the driver's seat, he wishes to evict not just Christian faculty but even students who do not subscribe to his atheistic views. Ask any Christian academician how careful Christian *professors* need to be about acknowledging their faith in a classroom. Now Dawkins and others want the *students* to be silenced as well. Underneath their dangerous political correctness is an agenda to stifle all thought but their own.

We Cannot Remove Pain—the Felt Reality of Evil—from This World

I want to state an important truth from within the Christian worldview at this point. By removing pain from the human experience, Sam Harris is, in effect, trying to remove the *felt* reality of evil. There is one fundamental difference between God allowing a death to take place and me taking another life: God has the power to restore life; I don't. The story of evil is one part of a greater narrative. To ignore the greater narrative is to continue to raise particulars without accepting the general. In fact, there is no option left but to say there is no such thing as evil and there should be no such thing as pain. Psychiatry, in fact, is wrestling with the ramifications of a drug that removes guilt and remorse. What kind of a world will we have when a rapist can take a morning-after pill?

Some time ago, I read an article about a three-year-old girl in Elk River, Minnesota, who suffers from a rare malady that involves insensitivity to pain. It is called CIPA—Congenital Insensitivity to Pain with Anhidrosis. People with this disease feel no pain, nor do they sweat or shed tears. There are only approximately one hundred known cases in the world. Little Gabby Gingras has to be watched over constantly. At four months of age, her parents noticed that she would bite her own fingers till they bled, with no expression of discomfort. When she was two years old, she had to have her teeth re-moved to prevent her from biting herself and caus-ing serious injury. She could put her hand on a hot plate and burn herself without feeling a twinge of pain. She always has to wear safety glasses because in one instance she scratched her cornea badly. She plays sports with absolute fearlessness, never hesitant about banging into anything. She says she sometimes feels like crying, but she can't. The life of this little one is in perpetual danger. The average life span for a child with this malady is twenty-five years. The parents of children with CIPA have one prayer—that their child would feel pain.

If it is possible in our finite world with our lim-ited knowledge to be able to appreciate just one ben-efit of pain, is it not possible that God has designed this awareness within us to remind us of what is good for us and what is destructive? As horrendous as the illustrations may sometimes be, can we not see the moral framework that detects atrocities and resists tragedies? Could there be a greater, deeper answer than simply saying there is no God?

It was another atheist, O. Hobart Mowrer, who went on record as saying that by denying the reality of sin, we have, in effect, lost our way as human beings and now find ourselves groping in the dark for a definition of the meaning of life.

Denying the existence of God leads us to prepos-terous conclusions so that, in the end, the amoral world of the skeptic who simply cannot explain good is worse than the world of the theist who has an explanation for evil. This, as I see it, is at the root of our differences. Harris simply denies the condition of the human heart, in spite of abundant evidence to the contrary. I recall Malcolm Muggeridge once having remarked that the depravity of the human heart is at once the most intellectually resisted yet most empirically verifiable reality. Wickedness is always excused as anything but the moral degeneracy that has resulted from each one of us becoming the god of God.

The Human Heart Is Bent toward Evil

Do you want empirical evidence that the heart of mankind is naturally bent toward evil? Witness the atrocities we see around us in our world! We cannot keep blaming this "ism" and that "ism." The decisions and actions of each individual are determined by what is important to that individual.

And be careful not to judge a philosophy by its abuse. The difference between someone who calls himself or herself a Christian and yet kills and slaughters and an atheist who does the same thing is that the Christian is acting in violation of his or her own belief, while the atheist's action is the legitimate outworking of his or her belief.

Do you remember what Karl Marx said? He would have been proud of Sam Harris's metaphysical moorings on religion, for he tried the same thing Harris is trying. Marx said that religion is "the opium of the people." Yes, everybody who hates religion remembers this quote. But they forget, deliberately or otherwise, what Marx said in continuation of that thought: "Religion is the sigh of the oppressed creature, the heart of a heartless world, the soul of soulless conditions. It is the opium of the people.... Religion is only the illusory sun which revolves around man as long as he does not revolve around himself." Atheists want us to revolve around ourselves—no, even more, to revolve around their fluctuating philosophies.

How Do We Define Love?

Based on atheism's theory of origin, the death of meaning and the death of moral reasoning are guaranteed. What else is jettisoned? Love.

What would be an atheist's definition of love, may I ask? Is this also the product of glands, just as evil is nothing more than dancing to one's DNA, according to Richard Dawkins? Let me tell you a story I heard growing up.

India is a culture where many values are taught through parables and proverbs. Here is one such parable—the story of a young man in a certain village who fell in love with a woman in another village. His love for her was real, while she was just toying with him. One day she suggested to him that if he really wanted to marry her, he should prove that he loved her with a greater love than he had for anyone else. His response was, "Of course I love you more than I love anyone else!"

"Not so," she replied, "because you love your mother more than you love me."

He found her response quite ludicrous and tried to explain to her that his love for his mother was different from his love for her. But she would have none of it. "Unless you are willing to kill your mother and bring me her heart as the trophy of my victory, I will not agree to marry you," she declared.

The young man went home deeply troubled and completely confused. One day, in a fit of desperation to win this girl, he took a knife and killed his mother. Ripping her heart out of her body, he clenched it in his hand and ran the few miles to her village to present it to his girlfriend. But as he was running through the woods, he suddenly stumbled and fell, and the heart bounced out of his hand. On all fours now, pushing aside the underbrush and searching desperately for the heart, he began to panic. Frantic, he rolled aside a rock, and there was the heart lying behind it. With great relief, he picked it up carefully with one hand. As he rose to his feet, dusting the dirt from the knees of his pants with his other hand, he heard a voice coming from the heart, saying, "Son, are you hurt? Son, are you hurt?"

When I first heard that story as a little boy, no one needed to explain it to me. I knew it was declaring that the love of a mother is so powerful that no betrayal can thwart it. It is always interesting that whenever I have told this story in Asian and Latin American countries, somebody inevitably comes to me and says, "We have a similar parable in our culture."

How is it that out of "nothing" we end up with such profound illustrations of a mother's heart? Didn't Bertrand Russell say at the end of his life that his longing for love had governed his life? Why do the songwriters in our society, more than anything else, write of that same recurring theme? Love is the longing of the human heart in the most majestic terms.

USA Today reported the true story of Geary and Mary Jean Chancey, who went to their watery graves when the train they were traveling on crashed into the swirling waters near Mobile, Alabama—but not before they had pushed their eleven-year-old daughter, Andrea, out of a window into the arms of a woman who had been traveling in the same car. Andrea, who has cerebral palsy and uses a wheelchair, survived with the help of the woman and others around them.

Where does this kind of sacrificial love come from? This is what a philosopher would call a "supererogatory act," a morally good act that goes well above and beyond the call of duty. May I suggest to you that the Chanceys risked their lives as the stronger to protect the weaker, which completely goes against natural selection. God forbid that such a "weak" one would be left at the mercy of Sam Harris's worldview, the ethical imperatives of which are espoused unblushingly by the Peter Singers of this world (professor of philosophy at Princeton), who believe that a pig is of more value than a child who has a disability! The ultimate test of any civilization is what we do with our children, and our children are not doing very well. From abortion to child pornography, atheistic philosophy is having its way with our children.

Is Secular Western Europe Better Off Than North America?

I must add one more thing here. Sam Harris talks often about the advances of countries less religious than ours, such as the countries of Western Europe (see *Letter*, xi, 43–46). Has he seen the exploitation of sex in Europe? A single stroll through some of their airports will reveal what is available to the perverted. And in the United States if it weren't for the influence of the gospels of Luke and Matthew regarding the virgin birth, we could have had the same thriving sex industry and poured billions into the economy of less fortunate countries, just by using their attractive women. Yes, you read that correctly. According to Harris, the story of the virgin birth of Jesus recorded by Luke and Matthew is the reason for Western sexual inhibitions (see *Letter*, 58).

Has Harris seen the trafficking of young women funneled into the cesspool of Amsterdam's red-light district? My daughter works in the rescue of women in the sex-trafficking industry. Europe is a nightmare where young women are in the vise-like grip of this horrific trade. I could tell you story after story, but let me tell you just one. A woman who works with a Christian group that rescues children from the clutches of sex traffickers told me that in one instance she rescued an eighteen-month-old baby girl from the arms of a man getting his sexual thrills with that child.

Do you know that these people who live according to atheistic philosophy and run these places threaten the lives of those such as my daughter who are trying to rescue such children? Where are Sam Harris and Richard Dawkins in all of this? Writing books about God's inaction perhaps? Has Harris studied the effects of pornography and its devastation in these countries that are "much better" (far healthier and less dysfunctional [see *Letter*, 43–44]) than "religious" America? It seems that his empirical quotient does not have such calibrations in it. In the end, his worldview will kill the majesty of love as well. Pragmatism will reign and moral commitments to fidelity will disappear.

Hope

What else dies in atheism? Hope.

If there's one recurring theme I have heard in my three decades of traveling the world, it is the longing of the human heart for hope. Devoid of reasons for hope, people will create substitutes and follow cultic rituals they have devised in anticipation of realizing hope.

What is Sam Harris's answer for hope in the ultimate stage of hopelessness, which is the way death is often seen? Nothing. Silence. The atheists' treatment of the subject of death is usually replete with debunkings of descriptions of "near death experiences," intended to dismiss any reality offered by the dying to those they are leaving behind. But how do they know these descriptions aren't true? One cannot, of course, just take utterances at face value, and so their skepticism is justified. But does it follow that oblivion or agnosticism is the only option?

This same kind of skepticism resided in some of the disciples, who did not believe at first that Jesus had risen from the dead. They had heard this kind of story before. They, too, had no clear understanding of what follows death and thought that perhaps Jesus' resurrection was some fanciful story conjured up by hallucinating women. I wonder whether multiple evidences that Jesus had risen from the dead, given to modern-day atheists, would make any difference. The apostle Peter saw more and was close to more of the miracles than almost any other disciple, yet when it mattered most, his faith struggled to survive.

The Need for Faith

The problem with evidence is that it is very much limited to the moment and creates the demand for more evidence. I have seen this in my own life over and over. Today it may be a failing business that is in need of God's intervention. Tomorrow I may want to be healed from cancer. The day after that, I may even want a loved one to be brought back from the dead.

The worldview of the Christian faith is simple enough. God has put enough into this world to make faith in him a most reasonable thing. But he has left enough out to make it impossible to live by sheer reason alone.

The teaching of the resurrection caught even the disciples by surprise, for they did not expect this dramatic turn. Their entire hope was politically based—that Jesus would somehow overthrow Rome. But a political victory would have been just as superficial a solution as Harris's solution for slavery and racism. Freedom that is granted only by law will not ensure that a former master sees his former slave as his equal.

A Different Hope

I was saddened to read Sam Harris's comments about the significant percentage of the prison population in France who are Muslims (*Letter*, 43–44), inferring that Western Europe wouldn't have a crime problem if not for its Muslim (or other religious) residents. As Scott Atran notes, "The obvious inference ... is that Islam encourages criminal behavior." Atran goes on to say, "What is not reported is that Muslims in the U.S. are as *underrepresented* in prison populations, as are U.S. Jews, and that the predictive factors for Muslims entering European prisons are almost exactly the same for African-Americans entering U.S. prisons, namely, lack of employment, schooling, political representation, and so forth. Moreover, religious education is a *negative* predictor of Muslims entering European prisons."

Sam Harris betrays a rather amazing prejudice. How he has gotten away with making slanderous statements in his book—accusing Muslim communities of "misogyny, their anti-Semitism, ... forced marriages, honor killings, punitive gang rapes, and a homicidal loathing of homosexuals"—boggles the mind (see *Letter*, 84). If he had said the same things about African-Americans, he would have found no publisher or institution willing to employ him. Using his same argument, he may as well say that the problem in the world is males—if we could just eliminate all males under twenty-five, we would have a better world.

Has Harris seen the tinderbox of angst among these youth in France? Theirs is a breeding ground for crime and rioting. Shame on him for his callous statements and for the pathetic misrepresentations he employs in his hostility to a people and their beliefs!

I am not a Muslim, nor am I sympathetic to many Islamic doctrines. But I do understand the anger that builds up among youths in Pakistan and France and other places. Their rebellion, often a cry for a decency and respect they are rarely shown, has too often been exploited by murderous, hate-filled men. Sadly, writers like Harris add fuel to that fire of prejudice. Over the years I have been privileged to be the guest of Muslim universities and countries. They recognize that my beliefs are different from theirs, but they appreciate the respect with which I address their audiences. The disrespectful way in which Harris has addressed Muslims makes me wonder whether, if he were to make these same statements publicly in a Muslim country, he would leave unscathed. His prejudice is recognizable a mile away, and the mutual antipathy is literally a dead end.

Why has Harris gone this route? Is he not qualified to address the issues between us apart from the method of calling for the eradication of belief? Or is it possible that he is trying to use the value of shock to propagate his views? Can he not see that his method is no different from some of the methods he is criticizing?

May I suggest that Muslim radicals are employing the same rancor Harris does because they have been taught that this present world is the arena in which to settle all scores. And this approach stands in stark contrast to the teaching of Jesus, who spoke of a hope that did not need to be hidden or relinquished. He spoke of a hope that respected the body and the soul. He spoke of hope based in a relationship with God.

That which atheists find grotesque because of their pseudo-intellectualism, Jesus spoke of with great clarity. He spoke kindly yet directly to the woman at the well with five broken marriages and did not rail on her as if she were a renegade. The woman restored to health after having seven demons cast out of her by Jesus would be embarrassed by the shamelessness of Hollywood and what they have made of her commitment to Jesus. Whether by means of *The Last Temptation of Christ* or *The DaVinci Code*, somehow this Mary Magdalene is dragged into the private life of the skeptic's imagination. Those in the entertainment industry who worship sex haven't the faintest understanding of the tenderness and affection Jesus had for women who were so marginalized in their time. They cannot even recognize Jesus' touch of purity.

Given a starting point of primordial slime, one is forced to live apart from a moral law, with no meaning, no real understanding of love, and no hope.

The Two Tests of Pascal's Wager

If Sam Harris is wrong, there is no second chance for him to get it right. This is where, in a conversation with author and pastor Rick Warren in *Newsweek* magazine, Harris missed the point of Pascal's wager. The French philosopher Blaise Pascal didn't say he was wagering his belief. He was essentially saying that there are two tests for belief: the empirical test—that which is based on investigation—and the existential test—that which is based on personal experience. By denying the existence of God, Harris leaves himself just one option in his pursuit of happiness and purpose, namely, the existential test of self-fulfillment.

For the believer in God and the follower of Jesus, there is more than the existential test, which is subject to circumstance and condition. We also have the empirical test of the person, teaching, and work of Jesus Christ. Atheists may respond by saying there is an empirical test for the naturalist as well, one who believes in matter alone. But on issues of morality and meaning they have nothing to look to for a moral framework beyond themselves, and if their assumptions are true, the existential arena is the only legitimate route for the pursuit for meaning. Pascal was declaring that if the existential test for finding meaning in life was the only option left to him, the hungers of his heart had been met in following Jesus and thus he was fulfilled. In a worst-case scenario, where the atheist is right and death is oblivion, Pascal had still met the only test the atheist has for belief and had found his relationship with Jesus to be existentially fulfilling. As a Christian, he met both his own test for truth in the person of Jesus—the empirical test—*and* the existential test posed by the atheist. It was for that reason he could say he could not be a loser, and the gamble was not a gamble he could lose, no matter which test he used.

Fleeting Pleasures, or Ultimate Justice?

In his follow-up to the dialogue with Rick Warren, Sam Harris's misunderstanding of Pascal was again on display. Harris suggested that "there are many questionable assumptions built into this famous wager. One is the notion that people do not pay a terrible price for religious faith.... What have been the psychological costs imposed by Christianity's anxiety about sex these last seventy generations? The current costs of religion are incalculable."

Did he once again miss a whole world of moral reasoning and unwittingly betray an underlying hedonism? Is that his endgame? Get rid of the moralizers so that we can clear the playing field? His argument from this narrow perspective is saying, in essence, that to forfeit ultimate justice beyond the grave is no big loss because of the momentary pleasures of existence in the here and now. Believing this would make the Hitlers and Stalins of history who died without being brought to justice the real winners.

Think of a world where there is no ultimate justice! Think of young Seung-Hui Cho, a student at Virginia Tech University, who slaughtered thirty-two students and professors and then shot himself. He has won in a world where there is no ultimate justice. Innocent people have been randomly shot, and their families have no recourse and no closure. Are you at peace with that? Does it make sense for Harris to be more concerned that the Christian may lose out on some sensual pleasure than with the loss of ultimate justice, which Aristotle called the core ethic? And as for forfeiting pleasures, I have talked to the indulgent and have seen that they have come away empty.

Apart from a moral framework, pleasure is a sure path to sensual bankruptcy. No, the Christian who enjoys legitimate pleasure within God's boundaries experiences life as a perpetual novelty. The boundary-less life of sensual pleasure is a field of landmines, fraught with the real risk that even the very possibility of pleasure might be blown away.

Jesus said, "I have come that they may have life, and have it to the full" (John 10:10). He didn't talk just about the way to live; he argued principally for the *truth* by which to live. The objective informs the subjective. Pascal was a thinker, and he reminded his readers that the mind and the heart—the empirical and the existential—have to be connected. Sadly, Harris misses this truth.

The Christ of Scripture

Let me move on to the appalling statements made by Sam Harris about the person of Jesus. The *pièce de résistance* of his book comes on page 58, where he says that though the writers of the gospels of Luke and Matthew cite the Greek rendering of Isaiah 7:14 as the basis for their declaration that Mary conceived as a virgin, it is based on a "mis-translation" of the original Hebrew text of Isaiah. The Hebrew word that Isaiah uses is *almah*, which Harris says "simply means 'young woman,' without any implication of virginity." Thus, he says, "the dogma of the virgin birth, and much of the Christian world's resulting anxiety about sex," is due to a mistake.

As I reread this paragraph, I had to wonder how his editor did not caution him against such plain nonsense. Mr. Harris is an intelligent man. Where did he come up with such convoluted reasoning — the Christian world's "anxiety about sex" has resulted from its belief in the virgin birth, which is based on a mistranslation of this Hebrew text?

A few lines later, Harris states that Paul doesn't even mention the virgin birth in his writings. Since Harris sees a direct link between belief in the virgin birth (which Paul does not mention) and anxiety over sex, how does he account for Paul's "anxiety" about sex, since most of the teaching we have in the Bible against sexual promiscuity comes from Paul? How did the "mistranslation" of a Hebrew text affect Paul's teaching on sexual purity when Paul never mentions the supposed source of anxiety?

Harris also comments on the apostle John's apparent discomfort with the "accusations of Jesus' illegitimacy" and John's failure to mention "his miraculous origins" (*Letter*, 58). Yet nobody gives a more glorious picture of Jesus than John in his apocalyptic vision. He was hardly embarrassed or uncomfortable with Jesus' divinity, so why would it be difficult for him to accept the virgin birth? Besides, John saves some of his most scorching words against sexual immorality for the meeting between the promiscuous and God. Where, then, does his "anxiety about sex" come from if, according to Harris, he was uncomfortable with the teaching of the virgin birth?

What does one say to such illogicality? My mother used to quote a Tamil proverb that said, "He got bumped from the rear, but his teeth fell out," meaning, "What's the connection?"

It's all too clear that Harris is not a biblical scholar and that he should have read further into Isaiah. Has Harris ever studied the very complexity of this subject? Is he aware of the nature of Hebrew prophecy and its genre? Does he know that there are numerous examples of Hebrew prophecies that have a "compenetration" of two fulfillments—one in part and the other in whole? This is so in 2 Samuel 7, which refers in its fulfillment to both David and the Messiah; the same is true in Psalm 2. It is a common technique in Hebrew prophecy. The Hebrews understood compenetration and how it worked, and Matthew was a Hebrew.

If Isaiah had used the typical Hebrew word for virgin, *betulah*, it would have been the wrong word for the situation. The immediate fulfillment of the prophecy comes in Isaiah 8:3, when Isaiah's wife gives birth to a son. The people had asked for a sign that God would indeed send the Messiah, and the birth of Isaiah's son was the immediate sign that the greater prophecy and promise of the virgin birth would be fulfilled. After all, what good to them would a sign be that wasn't given until seven hundred years later? So Isaiah used the word *almah*, which is literally translated "young maiden" and *can* include virginity. Therefore, it is the very word he needed in order to cover both situations—that of Isaiah's wife and of Joseph's fiancée, Mary.

But even more to the point, the doctrine of the virgin birth is based on Mary's own admission. Joseph wished to end his marital contract with Mary because he was perplexed until the angel appeared to him and verified Mary's story. By religious law he would have had to go to the scribe and publicly declare that this was not his child. Is Harris as willing to acknowledge what Isaiah has written (9:6)—"For to us a child is born, to us a son is given, and the government will be on his shoulders. And he will be called Wonderful Counselor, Mighty God, Everlasting Father, Prince of Peace"—to support Jesus' divinity as he is to use Isaiah 7 to debunk the virgin birth? He is grasping at straws when he stoops to such poor argumentation.

The Nature of Prophecy

Sam Harris's treatment of Matthew 27:9–10 regarding the "thirty silver coins" also reveals his ignorance on the subject of biblical prophecy (see *Letter*, 58). He says that Matthew credits Jeremiah with the prophecy of the thirty pieces of silver when, in fact, it comes from Zechariah. Harris either didn't know or didn't go to the trouble to explain that there are two passages of scriptural prophecy that converge into this one fulfillment of the thirty silver coins. Jeremiah 19 mentions a potter and a "field" that is called the "Valley of Slaughter" (verse 6), which in Matthew 27:8 is called "the Field of Blood." That field under that name, where the Bible says that Judas hanged himself and was buried, still exists to this very day. Jeremiah's focus is on the innocent blood that was shed (Jeremiah 19:4). Zechariah specifically mentions that the price of *betrayal* was thirty pieces of silver (Zechariah 11:12). The New Testament writer Matthew tells us that the innocent man whose blood was shed was Jesus, and for betraying him Judas received thirty pieces of silver. Matthew refers to Jeremiah's writing because the actual price of redemption was the blood that was shed rather than the silver Judas was paid.

Does Harris really expect to take one line out of the twenty thousand lines in the New Testament and consider it evidence on which to debunk the totality of its message? On that basis, we should not trust science as a discipline or give scientists any authority whatsoever, considering how many billions of years' difference there is among physicists and astronomers in estimates for the age of the earth. These margins are allowed, knowing the data from which they are selectively drawing.

Harris's complaint that the Bible is not more specific in mathematics is straining at a gnat and swallowing a camel. For example, he points out that Scripture (1 Kings 7:23–26; 2 Chronicles 4:2–5) states that "the ratio of the circumference of a circle to its diameter is 3:1" (*Letter*, 61). But mathematical formulas is not what the Bible is about. When did you last see an organic chemistry book talk about marriage? After all, shouldn't there be some chemistry between a husband and wife? But exploring "relational" chemistry is not the purpose of the study of organic chemistry. Why didn't Harris look at how detailed Daniel 11 is in its prophecy of the next three hundred years? Perhaps because if he found Daniel too convincing, he would feel compelled to show that someone like Nostradamus also made predictions that came true.

Harris reminds me of a certain psychiatric patient who kept insisting that he was dead. After many long hours the doctors finally convinced him that only living people bleed. Immediately they jabbed a needle into him, and as he saw blood spurting out, he cried, "Good grief! I guess dead people bleed too!"

God on Trial for Evidence of His Existence

It appears that no matter what evidence was offered, God could never prove himself to Sam Harris because it's not proof he is looking for. He is looking for a God he has cast in his own image. And he is certainly not the first to ask God to stoop to providing proof of himself according to another's agenda. Centuries ago, Satan said to Jesus, "Turn these stones into bread." "Throw yourself down from this pinnacle and see if God will keep you from hurting yourself." "Worship me, and I'll give you world dominion" (see Matthew 4:3, 6, 9). It seems to me that the gospel writers understood the likes of atheists better than atheists understand themselves or, should I say, better than atheists *care to* understand themselves. Those of us who have spent half our lives wrestling with these kinds of arguments recognize hostility for what it is and know when arguments go beyond the boundaries of what is believable. Let me give you a couple of examples.

In Buddhism There Is No Self

Any time Sam Harris sees something good about what Jesus said or did, he dismisses it with a sentence or two or compares it to something found in some other religion he finds superior. His self-described method of selecting a passage from Buddhist literature at random and opening the page "with closed eyes" couldn't be more reflective of his entire approach (see *End of Faith*, 216). He is clearly out of his depth here. Here is a portion of the passage he has chosen from the writings of Padmasambhava, the founder of Tibetan Buddhism:

> *In the present moment, when [your mind] remains*
> *in its own condition without constructing*
> *anything,*
> *Awareness at that moment in itself is quite*
> *ordinary.*
> *And when you look into yourself in this way*
> *nakedly [without any discursive thoughts],*
> *Since there is only this pure observing, there will be*
> *found a lucid clarity without anyone being there*
> *who is the observer;*
> *Only a naked manifest awareness is present.*

By his own admission, Harris took the book off the shelf and randomly opened it to this passage to illustrate his point of the superiority of Eastern spirituality over Judaism, Christianity, and Islam—all of which he admits emphasize faith over the empirical mysticism of Hinduism and Buddhism.* After quoting this random passage of Buddhist literature, he concludes that "one could live an eon as a Christian, a Muslim, or a Jew and never encounter any teachings like this about the nature of consciousness" (*End of Faith*, 216).

He is absolutely right. And do you know why a person would never encounter anywhere else teachings like those of Buddhism about the nature of consciousness—a "naked manifest awareness"? It is because, unlike Judaism, Christianity, Islam, or even Hinduism, Buddhism doesn't believe in the existence of the individual self. There is no "I" or "you." There is no observer or "selfs" to observe.

Harris's selective use of religious teachings warrants the charge of "special pleading," the violation of a law of logic that requires that the same rules apply to both sides of the argument. Given the way he has used these teachings, I can't help but wonder whether he even understands them—and if he does understand them, he has done an even greater disservice.

In fact, Gautama Buddha would not have appreciated Harris's compliment. He would have placed Harris at the bottom rung of his ladder because

---

* "Faith," Harris writes, "is rather like a rhinoceros, in fact: it won't do much in the way of real work for you, and yet at close quarters it will make spectacular claims upon your attention" (*End of Faith*, 215).

if there's one thing that comes through in Harris's books, it is passion, will, power, desire—the very things Buddha considered to be the source of all suffering. The fact that Harris even desired to write *The End of Faith* runs afoul of the "soul" of Buddhism, because Buddha denied the existence of individuality for the same reason that Harris is nontheistic. The very foundation of Harris's scientific approach is built on the basis of an observer—which doesn't exist in Buddhism, or at least ought not to exist. Belief in God necessarily means a belief in the individuality of every person. Isn't it fascinating that an argument that started as the denial of God ends with the denial of self? The mass murderer at Virginia Tech University used a question mark in reference to his name. The logical outworking of the denial of God is to question the worth of every individual.

I dare Harris to revise his book in a way that is true to Buddhism, devoid of the use of personal pronouns. Because for *him* to write a book to tell *me* that what *Buddha* teaches is better than anything either *Jesus* or *Muhammad* ever taught involved five individuals in order for him to make his point—none of whom actually have an individual self, according to Buddhist teaching.

The Harm of Jainism

Sam Harris reveals a similar lack of understanding about Jainism when he addresses what he judges to be the positives about that belief system. He says he finds Jainism utterly harmless as compared to the horrible things that Christianity has done and that Jainism has a superior ethic to Christianity (see *Letter*, 11–12). Does he know that Mahavira, a great teacher of Jainism, wore a mask over his mouth so that he wouldn't swallow any insects, which are only different in degree to what he thinks a human being to be? If Jainism's ethic is superior, the next time Harris sits down for dinner, out of regard for his next of kin, he should pass on the steak.

Harris also observed that Martin Luther King Jr.'s inspiration came from Gandhi (see *Letter*, 12). It might surprise Harris to know that Mahatma Gandhi thought much more highly of Jesus than he does and, in fact, carried a New Testament with him everywhere he went. In the museum at Gandhi's ashram in Ahmedabad is a quote by Bertrand Russell, of all people, with his assessment of why Gandhi was successful in his campaign against British rule in India: "It is doubtful that the method employed by Gandhi would have ever succeeded, except that he was appealing to the conscience of a Christianized people." Here is an ardent atheist referring to a pantheist and saying that the only reason he succeeded in his goal of national independence was that he was appealing to the conscience of theists.

No matter how much Harris may try to disguise it, he is assuming a moral law he has no right to assume. He makes moral pronouncements on other religions as superior to Christianity by smuggling in an objective moral framework to which these religions would not subscribe, all the while totally ignoring the very foundations on which these religions stand and which actually diminish him, in stark distinction to the Christian faith. Hinduism has a caste system that's intrinsic to it. Buddhism denies personhood. Jainism puts him on a par with the insect world. A study of the code of Hammurabi or the Laws of Manu reveals a stark difference from Christianity in their starting points. Only in the Judeo-Christian teaching do ethical imperatives follow from human worth, which has been imparted by God, not by human beings.

The Inherent Morality of the Ten Commandments

When Sam Harris dismissively says that the first four commandments "have nothing whatsoever to do with morality" (*Letter*, 20), I can only shake my head in disbelief. He obviously isn't able to understand that the last nine hang on the first commandment, "I am the LORD your God, who brought you out of Egypt.... You shall have no other gods before me" (Exodus 20:2–3). Without the first one, none of the remaining nine commandments matter. When I quoted Harris's statement to an audience of young thinkers in the East, they responded with a visibly stunned look on their faces and even laughter. Whereas Harris could not, they were able to recognize the logical connection between the first commandment and the nine that follow it. This is the biggest difference between the atheist's moral framework and the Judeo-Christian framework.

In the statement "I am the LORD your God, who brought you out of Egypt," two precepts are being taught: (1) all moral reasoning is based on the actuality of God, and (2) "righteousness" or "morality" cannot be attained without redemption. Though Harris may see this as a totally foreign and bizarre concept, it is based on the soundest thinking and reflects reality. For the Hebrews, redemption always precedes righteousness, and worship is always preceded by redemption and righteousness. You cannot be righteous until you are first redeemed, and you cannot worship until you are redeemed and righteous. This sequence cannot be altered.

But to Harris as an atheist, worship is the curse on a humanity that has come of age. At the same time, he recognizes the tug on the human heart toward the sacred. Hence some of the irrational and bankrupt suggestions that come from within the ranks of atheism, such as Carolyn Porco's suggestion at the Salk Institute lectures that science create its own rituals and ceremonies to inspire awe. One of my friends once said he would never be an atheist because there are no holidays—well, Porco's solution should take care of that objection! Such attempts to manufacture awe are doomed to failure when they originate from a fake morality—and they lie at the root of the difference between the moral framework of every other religion and that of Christianity or Judaism.

But here the Christian faith stands alone. Consider the fascinating conversation between Jesus and self-righteous people trying to pit politics against religion:

> "Is it right for us to pay taxes to Caesar or not?" they asked.
> Jesus asked them for a coin. "Whose portrait and inscription are on it?" he asked.
> "Caesar's," came the answer.
> Jesus responded, "Then give to Caesar what is Caesar's, and to God what is God's."*

The questioners were very much like Sam Harris. Their only purpose for asking the question was the hope that they could trip Jesus up. Jesus' answer

---

* See Luke 20:22–25.

caught them off guard and should have forced another question from them. But they fell silent after the imperative of Jesus' answer showed up their hypocrisy. They ought to have followed up with the obvious question, "What belongs to God?"

And I strongly suspect that Jesus would have said, "Whose portrait and inscription are on you?"

On another occasion, Jesus' questioners tried to force him to pit one commandment against another. "Which is the greatest commandment," they asked him. The Mosaic precepts had 613 commandments. David reduced the core commandments to fifteen, Isaiah to six, and Micah to three. I would have thought Jesus would reduce them to one, but he didn't. He reduced them to two: " 'Love the Lord your God with all your heart and with all your soul and with all your mind.' ... And the second is like it: 'Love your neighbor as yourself' " (Matthew 22:37, 39).

Where can you find this in Buddhism, where there is no individual worth, no self, and no "other"? You see, from the first of the two commandments the second inextricably follows. Without the first, the second is merely prescriptive, without reason or basis. Jesus carried this further in the story of the Good Samaritan (see Luke 10:25–37). In that parable he focused on the outcast of society, who understood the divine imperative to care for our fellow human beings—including those who despise us—even better than did the priests and the Levites, with all their hard-earned knowledge.

Is Christianity to Blame for Slavery?

Sam Harris also takes Christianity to task over slavery, which I find highly ironic (see *Letter*, 14–19). On the surface he argues for equality of human worth (see *Letter*, 18). At the same time, he makes fun of the beliefs of billions of people and wants to eradicate those beliefs on the basis of his belief that the scientist who believes in matter alone is, in effect, intellectually superior. He says specifically that 93 percent of scientists do not accept the idea of God (see *Letter*, 39). Where does he get this figure? Which scientists is he talking about? Are they Western or Eastern, Communist or capitalist? What if a higher percentage of Eastern scientists believe in God than do Western scientists? Will that prove that Westerners are intellectually superior to Easterners? I have seen statistics declaring that as many as 40 percent of scientists do believe in God.

But even if Harris's figure is true, can't we argue that just because a high percentage of people believe something, it doesn't make that something morally correct? There is a reason that slavery is not directly addressed in the Bible, as Harris desires it to be. He evidently has not read Job 31:13–15, where Job argues for justice for those who work for him and that both he and they are equal in their humanity.

The New Testament contains a beautiful and tender letter written by Paul to Philemon, a slave owner, in which Paul asks him to deal with his runaway slave not as a servant but as a brother. In a key line, Paul writes, "I could be bold and order you to do what you ought to do" (verse 8), but he doesn't. Instead, he appeals not merely to the law of the land but to the higher law of love: "So if you consider me a partner, welcome him as you would welcome me. If he has done you any wrong or owes you anything, charge it to me" (verses 17–18). What more would Sam Harris like him to say?

In contrast to the egalitarianism that the Christian faith clearly teaches are the writings of renowned atheists *against* egalitarianism. Egalitarianism is not a tenet of atheism. Listen to Nietzsche: "Equality is a lie concocted by inferior people who arrange themselves in herds to overpower those who are naturally superior to them. The morality of 'equal rights' is herd morality, and because it opposes the cultivation of superior individuals, it leads to the corruption of the human species."

Here you have one of their own telling us that there are "superior" humans and "inferior" ones. We have been down the atheist road before, and it ended in a Holocaust. It was belief in an absolute morality, in true God-given egalitarianism, that brought slavery to an end. The reason Jesus was silent on the issue of slavery is very simple. He was silent on many issues that the "law" could have addressed without changing the heart, including the overthrow of Rome—the empire that had enslaved his own beloved Jerusalem and his people. His disciples wanted him to speak out against the laws of Rome, which exploited them and restricted the practice of their faith. In fact, those who wanted to silence Jesus even pitted Rome against him, but he still did not speak out against the Roman tyranny.

Jesus' Method for Changing Human Hearts

Jesus' method is a drastically different enforcement method. The "laws" of love and of inner impulse are different from the laws of science. Ask anyone who has ever loved another person. Jesus worked by changing the heart, not by legislating. Legislation can only force compliance. It can never produce the love necessary to change an attitude.

Jesus also spoke little about the breakup of a home. It was never his intent to encourage a breakup of the home. The provision for divorce was made because of the hardness of human hearts (see Matthew 19:8). True goodness flows from a change of heart and from the outflow of love, not from the threat of punishment. That truth, by the way, is why even the horror of hell is more the outcome of a heart that seeks to disown God and play God and live eternally with those who do the same than it is retribution against evil. C. S. Lewis once wrote that "there are only two kinds of people in the end: those who say to God, 'Thy will be done,' and those to whom God says, in the end, '*Thy* will be done.'"

Slavery is illegal now, but is *racism* gone? Gandhi tried to change the law of the caste system, and today the law protects those of the "lower castes." But do you really think discrimination in India against the lower castes is gone? The words of George Mac-Donald are appropriate: "To love righteousness is to make it grow, not to avenge it. Throughout his life on earth, Jesus resisted every impulse to work more rapidly for a lower good." Philip Yancey adds to MacDonald's thought: "Moral force, to be sure, is a risky form of power. Compared to the glaring reality of brute force, it may appear weak and ineffectual. But it has its own way of conquering."

On their own scientific terms, atheists should know that we do not change people's hearts by mocking them and castigating them. Sam Harris's entire approach toward banishing religious belief runs afoul of his own scientific premise. Those who study ends and means tell you that change does not come from such bullying.

The degree to which Harris has stooped in his derision of Mother Teresa (see *Letter*, 35–36) is reprehensible, in spite of the recent revelation of seasons of doubt in her life. (Which honest believing person has never struggled with doubt—even recurring doubt? It remains a fact, as she herself said, that her life was lived for the glory of God in spite of occasions of doubt about him or what he was doing.) This mockery of Teresa is borrowed from Christopher Hitchens, a man too intelligent to have written a book as base as *The Missionary Position* (the very title reveals the crassness of his mind). In an Internet conversation with Andrew Sullivan, journalist for *The Atlantic* magazine, Harris declared that an ethic of doing good that comes from one's own motivation is better than an ethic that comes from a desire to serve God and, therefore, your fellow man in need. So the natural conclusion is that Mother Teresa's ethic is inferior to Harris's. But Harris failed to add an important qualifier: his idea of "good" is that which comes from one's own motive—and in this case, it is in keeping with *Harris's* definition of good.

Apparently Harris is not aware that the Sisters of Charity serve the poor without seeking to convert them. I once asked Mother Teresa if the sisters and her workers talked about their Christian faith to the men and women they rescued. Much to my surprise, she said, "No, we just love them." She died leaving behind just a metal bucket for washing herself and two cotton saris. People of every stripe, including atheists, walked silently behind Mother Teresa's body to honor her because of her service to the destitute. Even the president of the world's most atheistic nation, Albania, told me she was a woman of extraordinary integrity and a stellar example in a hurting world. Harris and Hitchens have the audacity, sitting in the comfort of their own homes, to denigrate Teresa's life given over to serving millions of unloved people! I cannot help but wonder whether it is really evil that Harris has a problem with or whether it is just that goodness makes him feel uncomfortable.

Surely not everything Mother Teresa did or believed is in my comfort zone. But shame on me if I cannot recognize the power of a life so beautifully lived. People like Hitchens and Harris need to find a dartboard other than Teresa against which to hurl their sharp-tongued polemics. Because of the ill-disguised hatred behind their arguments, some of their readers are beginning to worry whether we are seeing the new brand of intellectual supremacists masquerading as spokespersons for pure science. We have been down this road before, and this fear is not without historical precedent.

Genetic Engineering: Mathematics of the Soul?

This brings me to one of Sam Harris's most forceful arguments—spread over the mysterious terrain of genetic engineering and human cloning. He acknowledges that the bottom-line argument for the difference between a fly, for example, and a blastocyst is the potential in the blastocyst to become a fully developed human being (see *Letter*, 30). He introduces the possibility of a three-day-old embryo possessing a soul and wonders whether an embryo that has split into twins has one soul split into two. And then he makes an incredibly profound statement: "Isn't it time we admitted that this arithmetic of souls does not make any sense?" (*Letter*, 31).

But isn't that precisely what he is doing in his support of genetic engineering and human cloning—making the embryo a zero and the adult a one? Isn't that precisely what he does when he wants to reduce human life to chemical equations?

Years ago, F. W. Boreham addressed this difference brilliantly in an essay titled "The Sword of Solomon." He reminded us that there is a plane on which mathematical propositions are approximately sound. But when you rise from that plane to a loftier one, they are untenable. Solomon proves it at the city gate (see 1 Kings 3:16–28). It may be true that half a dollar and half a dollar make one dollar; it is obviously untrue that half a baby and half a baby make one baby:

> Let the sword do its deadly work; let it cleave this baby into two parts, and half a baby plus half a baby will represent but the grim and gruesome mockery of a baby. When a man distributes his wealth among his children, he gives to each a part; but when a woman distributes her love among her children, she gives it all to each. I do not believe that any man who has once fallen in love will ever be persuaded that one and one are only two. He looks at her, and he feels that one plus one would be a million.

When you put your blade to the little entity of life, you are seeing mathematics at work. When God splits the embryo, we are seeing majesty at work that goes beyond the numerals. That is why a mother who has lost a child doesn't simply say, "Oh well, I can always have another one." We allow the majesty and the mystery of life and the marvel of individual "soul making" to remain in the hands of a Creator we have reasons to believe in. Harris, who believes only in the logic of mathematics, wants to reduce all of life to the logic of math. But when it comes to souls and his wish to transcend mathematics, he is caught in his own craftiness.

Life is not mathematics. Yet Harris wants the scientist and the mathematician to become sovereign over all of life. I am afraid that their track record is not very good. Listen to Richard Dawkins here:

> There was a well-known television chef who did a stunt recently by cooking human placenta and serving it up as a pate, fried with shallots, garlic, lime juice and everything. Everybody said it was delicious. The father had seventeen helpings. A scientist can point out, as I have done, that this is actually an act of cannibalism. Worse, since cloning is such a live issue at the moment, because the placenta is a true genetic clone of the baby, the father was actually eating his own baby's clone. Science can't tell you if it's right or wrong to eat your own baby's clone, but it can tell you that's what you're doing. Then you can decide for yourself whether you think it's right or wrong.

Is this the scientist to whom Harris wants us to entrust our values? A scientist who gives a father the privilege of eating his own offspring's clone, with garlic and lime juice for added flavor? It's very clever of Dawkins, isn't it? What he gives up with one hand, he grabs back with the other: *science can't tell you whether it's right or wrong, but it can tell you it's up to you.* Are these the kind of people to whom we should entrust ourselves and our children?

Abortion and the Moral Value of Human Life

Sam Harris uses the same argument when he tries to find justification for abortion (see *Letter*, 36–38). I am in total sympathy with the struggle of a doctor who has to choose between the life of a baby and the life of its mother, where the survival of one will take the life of the other. Such a decision must be an agonizing ordeal. But the struggle of a decision in the face of extreme possibilities does not legitimize the decision across the board or make it normative.

If a man breaks into my home and tries to rape a family member, I will feel compelled to take my baseball bat and knock him out. May I then take my baseball bat and walk around my neighborhood attacking any man at will because I want to minimize the possibility of rape? And you know what? I can prove to you that the fewer human beings there are, the better the possibility that we will have less suffering—so let's just eliminate half of humanity.

Yes, the issue of the value of life is about more than mathematics. Science is lame when it comes to moral decisions; it limps as it walks, lacking an absolute moral law for life's purpose.

They declare that for the good of humanity they will find cures through stem cell research, genetic engineering, and cloning. It's a claim we have heard before. So Harris writes against Christians, accusing us of standing in the way of finding future cures (see *Letter*, 28–32), while he is indifferent to the fact that millions of babies are aborted every year right now. Why isn't his voice raised against the evil that is happening now? He ought to be in hospitals and clinics every day, trying to prevent another abortion from taking place if, as he charges, even one death is inexcusable.

This is the world to which his philosophy is taking us. He wants to end suffering by means of stem cell research? To end suffering, did he petition his elected officials when they were considering partial birth abortions? One of the representatives of Harris's worldview, Supreme Court Justice Ruth Bader Ginsburg, has stated that to uphold the ban on partial birth abortion would be a denial of a woman's right.* To crush the head of her baby just because it is still in her womb is a woman's right? This is a step toward ending suffering?

Did Harris write to Peter Singer at Princeton to object to his view that a pig is worth more than a deformed child? My mother spent her life teaching

---

* In her dissent, Justice Ginsburg declared that the majority's opinion "cannot be understood as anything other than an effort to chip away a right declared again and again by this court, and with increasing comprehension of its centrality to women's lives." Quoted in Bill Mears, "Justices Uphold Ban on Abortion Procedure," *http://www.cnn.com/2007/LAW/04/18/scotus.abortion/index.html* (September 18, 2007).

"deformed" children. I saw what she accomplished in the precious lives of those whom Singer and Harris would implicitly demean. When these "deformed" little ones were informed of my mother's death, they wept because of their loss.

Has Harris expressed horror that female fetuses in India are being aborted over male fetuses at a ratio of ten to one? He extols Gandhi's nonviolent ethic. Is he bothered by the widespread and indiscriminate extermination of female lives in India? It seems to me that Harris's outrage has very little to do with the value of human life but everything to do with protecting *his* power and *his* value system. It is not Christians he is fighting; it is any authority that seeks to impose any parameters on his "freedom," while he cleverly tries to impose his own parameters on others. He lauds science as the discipline that deals with truth.

He says that every time we scratch our noses, we are committing the magnitude of another Holocaust because of the cells that are killed (see *Letter*, 30). He is serious when he says this. So I ask you, is that cell you just scratched off your nose the same as a blastocyst, or is it different? If it is the same, why aren't you content with adult stem cell research to help find cures? Ah, but there *is* a difference, isn't there?

There is a difference between a collection of cells and an organism that is equipped for integrated life. Is the alphabet the same thing as a work of poetry by Tennyson? Is paint and canvas the same thing as a painting by Rembrandt? This may be the central issue that divides us. To Sam Harris, a self-described atheist, human beings can be nothing more than their reducible chemicals. To believers in the person of Jesus, we are made in the image of God. Our sum total is greater than our parts. The blastocyst has everything needed to uninterruptedly produce human life, if nurtured.

Harris argues that if it is acceptable to harvest organs from a person who is brain-dead, why can't the brain-bereft blastocyst be used for experimentation (see *Letter*, 30)? The person who is brain-dead through age or natural causes, an accident, or a disease has no imminent potential. Harris wishes to cut short the immense potential for life of a human blastocyst by unnatural causes, by purposeful destruction, and by exalting violence. He is using the same kind of bizarre logic used by Senator Tom Harkin of Iowa when on the Senate floor, in support of embryonic stem cell research, he took out a pad of paper, put a dot on it and said, "What I've just put on that piece of paper is a dot, a little dot. That is the size of the embryos that we're taking the stem cells from." Does Senator Harkin remember that a dot is all he was when he started off? Should he therefore be flung onto a garbage heap if he becomes brain-dead some day? No, because the past tense of his life demands that we respect the future of his mortal remains. The past tense of every human being is that dot. We respect that life—that dot—for that very reason. In the same way, because of the "future tense" of a human blastocyst or embryo we respect that life—that dot.

Atheists and naturalists glorify the singularity from which this universe came. It's quite a dot, I must say! Even the period in a sentence means something. Why not that which envelops life? You may as well say that all language is just ink, that all music is just sound. Atheists seem to exercise their reductionistic tendencies selectively. If *religion* stands in the way of saving people, these people have infinite worth. But if the scientist stands in the way of preserving human life, the embryo is "nothing more than a dot." As the law of the excluded middle makes clear in philosophy, just because two things have one thing in common doesn't mean they have everything in common—and this dot means completely different things to astrophysics and biology.

The bottom line is this: Yes, stem cell research may yield some great benefits for us. Stem cells have the potential, after all, to become muscle, bone, skin, and a host of other body tissues. The question should be how we get such cells. Hans Keirstead and his team at the University of California have used *adult* stem cells with remarkable success. Bioethicist John Kilner has done excellent work in bringing sanity and caution into this debate by showing where and when adult stem cells entail fewer hazards and do not cross serious ethical lines.

As I am writing this, Shinya Yamanaka of Japan's Kyoto University has just announced a breakthrough in producing the equivalent of embryonic stem cells using the skin as a base and slipping four genes into the skin cells. The process, still in its early stages, is considered to be a huge step forward. So our whole discussion on embryonic stem cells versus adult stem cells may turn out to be moot.

The Moral Dangers of Cloning

I must go on to say some important things about Sam Harris's implicit assertion that only religious people (particularly Americans, whom he considers dinosaurs compared to progressive Europeans; see *Letter*, 43–46) have a strong bias against stem cell research and cloning. Far beyond stem cell matters, I consider the issue of cloning to be potentially more fearsome.

Harris must be aware that when the issue of human cloning was seriously debated a few years ago, the breadth of hostility toward it was noteworthy. Many leading proponents from the pro-choice position, representing many different disciplines and professions, including higher education (such as Princeton law professor Robert George), biotechnology, and journalism, spoke out strongly against the legalization of cloning, admitting that when it comes to cloning, we are talking about much more than abortion. Charles Krauthammer, journalist for *The Washington Post* who has served on the United States President's Council on Bioethics, has made this telling observation:

> Many secularly inclined people such as myself have great trepidation about the inherent dangers of wanton and unrestricted manipulation—to the point of dismemberment—of human embryos. You don't need religion to tremble at the thought of unrestricted embryo research. You simply have to have a healthy respect for the human capacity for doing evil in pursuit of the good.

The odds themselves are not in favor of successful cloning. In animals on which it has been tried, a pregnancy results only 3 to 5 percent of the time. And even in those rare cases when the pregnancy is carried to term, one-third die at birth or shortly thereafter. Others seem healthy at first, but in a short period of time it becomes apparent that they have heart and circulation problems, underdeveloped lungs, diabetes, immune system deficiencies, and severe growth abnormalities. Nigel Cameron, an expert in bioethics, and Lori Andrews, law professor and an expert in biotechnologies, have observed, "If an infectious disease were killing one-third of human infants, we would declare it a public health emergency. We certainly wouldn't set up a clinic to enable it to happen."

A powerful new coalition of groups you might never have expected to see—from feminists and the Catholic Church to conservative Republicans and liberal, if not libertarian, Democrats—cooperated in the public forum and before the United States Congress to make certain that their reservations about the direction genetic engineering might be taking us were brought into the debate. Many giving testimony against "therapeutic" cloning (the creation of cloned embryos in order to harvest stem cells) went to great lengths to make sure everyone knew they were coming from a perspective that was pro-choice on abortion. Yet they argued that cloning should be outlawed. Judy Norsigian of the Boston Women's Health Book Collective, an education and advocacy organization, spoke vehemently against all cloning, concluding, "The embryo is not nothing." If ever there were an understatement about human life, this is it.

It is surprising that the fight for cloning on the world scene is being led by Britain (the only country in the world where all options of cloning—using "spares" and creating and cloning embryos for research—are legal), initially under the leadership of former prime minister Tony Blair. I also find it interesting that Germany, which has been down this road before, banned all human cloning in 1990. In light of this, it is hardly accurate to state, as Harris has, that this is chiefly a concern of the Religious Right, nor is it fair to claim that Christian America is holding society back from achieving wonders for humanity (see *Letter*, 31–32).

The following observations by Nigel Cameron are powerful and dripping with an irony worth noting:

> This is not a debate about the freedom of science, or about abortion, and we certainly cannot allow it to become a debate about boosting the profits of the biotech industry. The importance of a clear moral framework to guide policy as we fast-forward into the momentous challenges of the biotech century is incalculable. Cloning has emerged as the flashpoint ethical question of our generation, a unifying force that draws together men and women of principle from across the cultural and political spectrum. We shall need to make a choice. Will Britain lead the way into the Brave New World, or shall we let the German conscience be our guide?

Truth: The Greatest Weapon

As I read Sam Harris's *Letter to a Christian Nation* and the way in which he portrays the triumph of science over the ignorance of religion, I thought of the words of Natan Sharansky, who was at one time the minister of internal affairs for Israel. Sharansky was imprisoned for many years under the yoke of the Russian gulag. Years later, when visiting the prison outside Moscow where he had been put into solitary confinement during the dark days of the Cold War, he asked if he could go into his old cell alone and spend a few minutes there. Then he brought in his wife and said to her, "This is where I found myself." Victimized by a brutal atheistic regime, he found harbor once again in realizing the value of every human life. It was not by accident that he then asked to go to the grave of the great Russian physicist Andrei Sakharov, who gave the Soviets the hydrogen bomb. As Sharansky addressed the media, he spoke of Sakharov's declaration that he had always thought the most powerful weapon in the world was the bomb, when in reality the most powerful weapon is the truth.

Think about it. If there is no God, then Sakharov is wrong in declaring that the truth is the most powerful weapon. If there is no God, then the most powerful weapon indeed must be the bomb, for it will destroy those who stand against you. The only way truth is more powerful than the bomb is if the destruction of one's life is not the end of that life. When the bomb was invented, all kinds of triumphalistic notions came to the fore. Those who gave us the bomb regret the ends to which it has now been used. If we sacrifice the sacredness of life and move forward with this goal of splitting human life in order to try to find cures for diseases, we may bring about a cloudburst of horror beyond what we have ever imagined.

As a teen growing up, I remember hearing King Crimson, a progressive rock band, singing lyrics written by Peter Sinfield: "Knowledge is a deadly friend when no one sets the rules. The fate of all mankind I see is in the hands of fools."

It's not just the poets who fear Harris's kind of world. This is why a day or two before Albert Einstein died, he and Bertrand Russell issued a joint statement in which they said, "We have found that [the experts] who know most are the most gloomy." Einstein also cautioned that God "does not throw dice." Make no mistake about it, Sam Harris is throwing dice, and we are the pawns in his kind of world.

An Argument
for the Existence of God

My entire response to the charges made by Sam Harris hinges on one reality, so I turn to the case for the existence of God and the person of Jesus in particular. I will borrow an argument—one of the least complicated from among the many—from a philosopher at the University of Southern California, Professor Dallas Willard. He takes a three-stage approach in his defense for the existence of God.*

Routinely, three tests for truth are applied: (1) logical consistency, (2) empirical adequacy, and (3) experiential relevance. When submitted to these tests, the Christian message meets the demand for truth. Willard's carefully constructed argument is posted on his website (*www.dwillard.org*), or you may read it in the book *Does God Exist?* In the following sections, I will briefly paraphrase the argument.

No Physical Entity
Explains Its Own Existence

In stage one, regardless of how physical, concrete reality is sectioned out, we end up with a state where the evidence of any physical entity explaining its

---

* No, these are not proofs. Proof for metaphysical assertions is a misuse of the term.

own existence is zero. That said, we come to a real situation of determining how many series of causes it takes to explain all of existence. We cannot have an infinite series of causes in time, starting from the present of any completed state and moving backward in search of an ultimate cause, because if the sequence were infinite, we would never arrive at the present. And as already mentioned, nothing in this physical universe can explain its own existence, i.e., something does not come from nothing. Therefore, in order for there to be something (and there is), there must be at least one state that is self-existent and does not derive its existence from something else. And it must be something nonphysical.

In this first stage of the argument, then, we have not posited a God; we have just posited a nonphysical entity that explains its own existence and is uncaused.

The Design Shows Intelligence

In stage two of his argument, Willard posits the argument *to design*. The argument here is not of aesthetic design but of intelligent specificity. It is important to distinguish between the two. If you walked onto a distant planet and saw a million stones in a perfect triangle, you could, of course, argue that over millions of years this formation could have randomly happened in a pleasantly aesthetic way.

To even have the capacity to reason this far and to recognize the aesthetics of the arrangement of stones requires certain components or raw material—the "alphabet" for life—that sets us apart from our environment. A can of alphabet soup dumped onto a table implies that somebody made that soup. You would absolutely deny that those shapes just happened to be in the soup. And if the letters fell out of the can in sequence every time, you would never even consider the possibility that it was accidental.

But suppose I took a trip to a distant planet and saw a crumpled piece of paper on which were written the words, "Hello, Ravi, did you bring some curry and rice with you?" I would not in a million years conclude that this note was produced by the laws of physics. That note would have had to have been the result of intelligence, not chance. In the same way, the "raw materials" that have resulted in this universe as we have it have been brought together simultaneously in the most amazing combinations—combinations too amazing to have just happened by accident. That is the argument *to design*.

In stage one, the argument was that no physical entity explains its own existence. Stage two gives a challenge to demonstrate one example of order coming from disorder. Now to stage three, which deals with the course of human events — historical, social, and individual.

Jesus in the Course of Human Events

A look at human history — and specifically at the person and work of Jesus Christ — shows why he was who he claimed to be and why millions follow him today. A comparison of Jesus, Muhammad, Krishna (if he ever actually lived), Buddha, and Mahavira quickly shows the profound differences in their claims and demonstrations. In fact, none I have mentioned here except Jesus even claimed to be divine. Krishna came the closest, but considering him in the context of the Vedas and the Gita, one cannot even be certain that he truly lived. It boils down to this: for the follower of Jesus Christ, the fact that the universe cannot explain itself, added to the obvious intelligence behind the universe, linked to the historical and experiential verification of what Jesus taught and did, make belief in him a very rational and existentially fulfilling reality.

Contrary to Harris's ridiculing claim that followers of Jesus Christ live in a world of hocus-pocus, I think the reverse is true. It is Harris's naturalism — his trust in scientific knowledge — that propagates a mystification of that worldview in which only matter exists. C. S. Lewis has made this observation:

> There is something which unites magic and applied science while separating both from the "wisdom" of earlier ages. For the wise men of old, the cardinal problem had been how to conform the soul to reality and the solution had been knowledge, self-discipline, and virtue. For magic and applied science alike the problem is how to subdue reality to the wishes of men: the solution is a technique.

The one thing Harris has left unaddressed is how to persuade the human heart to do, and to *want* to do, that which is true, good, and beautiful. Technological advance without virtue in the technician is the nuclear button in the hands of a madman.

The stages in the argument for the existence of God (as presented by Willard) and the application of tests of truth to the message of the Christian gospel and its existential implications make for a reasonable and coherent worldview.

Religion and
Radical Secularism

I close my letter with some thoughts on religion and Harris's world of radical secularism. I share his deep concern about the way the Muslim world is being commandeered by those who lay claim to its original intent. But I fear Islam for different reasons. Islam is a religion that is academically bankrupt, for it fails to meet the ordinary tests of truth. Those who critique it run the risk of being obliterated. How can a religion that claims that its prophet came to the entire world restrict its miracle to a language that is not spoken by the vast majority of the people of the world? How can a man whose own passions were so untamed gain the right to speak moral platitudes? I've written about this and other critiques of Islam elsewhere.* An honest Muslim open to considering these things will readily see that the "God" of the Koran is not the same God spoken of in the Old and New Testaments and that the edifice of Islam is built on a geopolitical worldview masquerading as a religion.

If Harris sees no difference between Islam and the Judeo-Christian bequest, I dare him to go to Saudi Arabia or Iran (or any Islamic country) and deliver his talks there. If he wants empirical

* See especially *Jesus among Other Gods* (Nashville: Nelson, 2000).

evidence for the difference between the two systems, let him go and test it out. Islam is a religion of power; the Christian faith is one of communion and relationship with the One who made us.

I plead with society to allow the diversity of religious beliefs to be heard in the marketplace of public dialogue. Let the individual weigh the facts for himself or herself and see where the truth lies.

True Unity in Diversity

The greatest search in philosophy has been the search for unity in diversity. Out of this search has come the founding of universities. The Christian heartily sees unity in diversity in time, in other people, and in himself.

In *The End of Faith*, Sam Harris makes fun of the Eucharist (see *End of Faith*, 72–73), so may I explain why it is sublime and beyond any of the crassness Harris attributes to it. Only in worship that is offered both in spirit and in truth can the heart, mind, conscience, imagination, and will be brought to coalesce with high respect for both the flesh and the spirit. This was symbolized in the Eucharist as touch and taste, as the transcending meaning of the Eternal was brought into the temporal. This very act gives meaning to history. The apostle Paul wrote, "Whenever you eat this bread and drink this cup [now], you proclaim the Lord's death [the past] until he comes [the future]" (1 Corinthians 11:26).

The Eucharist brings unity within the diversity of every nation, language, and tongue. Paul reminded the Athenians that all people are of one family, no matter what their nationality (see Acts 17:24–28). The apostle John tells us that heaven's residents will be comprised of men and women "from every tribe and language and people and nation" (Revelation 5:9) taking part in the ultimate communion with God.

Science and religion do not have to be enemies; they are facets of one truth, whose source is God. Dr. John Polkinghorne, Anglican priest and former professor of mathematical physics, ends his book *One World* with these profound observations:

> Reality is a multi-layered unity. I can perceive another person as an aggregation of atoms, an open biochemical system in interaction with the environment, a specimen of *homo sapiens*, an object of beauty, someone whose needs deserve my respect and compassion, a brother for whom Christ died. All are true and all mysteriously coinhere in that one person. To deny one of these levels is to diminish both that person and myself, the perceiver; to do less than justice to the richness of reality. Part of the case for theism is that in God the Creator, the ground of all that is, these different levels find their lodging and their guarantee. He is the

source of connection, the one whose creative act holds in one the worldviews of science, aesthetics, ethics and religion, as expressions of his reason, joy, will and presence.

This interlocking character of the world of creation finds its fullest expression in the concept of sacrament, an outward and visible sign of an inward and spiritual grace, a wonderful fusion of the concerns of science and theology. Thus in the Eucharist, bread and wine which, in the words of liturgy, "earth has given and human hands have made," become the body and the blood of Christ, the source of spiritual life. The greatest sacrament, compared to which all the others are types and shadows, is the Incarnation in which "the Word became flesh and dwelt among us, full of grace and truth; we have beheld his glory, glory as of the only Son from the Father" (John 1:14 [RSV]). The Word, the *logos*, combines two notions, one Greek, one Hebrew. For the Greek the *logos* was the rational ordering principle of the universe. For the Hebrew the word of the Lord was God's activity in the world. [In Hebrew *dabar* means both word and deed. Hebrew is a language based on verbs, on action.] Science discerns a world of rational order developing through the unfolding of process, a fusion of Greek and Hebrew insights. Theology declares the world in its scientific character to be an expression of the Word of God. For "all things were made through him, and without him was not anything made that was made" (John 1:3 [RSV]).

I want to share with you what I said to a co-founder of Hamas in his home in the West Bank town of Ramallah as he railed against America's pursuit of sensual pleasures and its commitment to science and the material world alone: "Sheikh, not far from here, about five thousand years ago, Abraham took his son to the top of a mountain to offer him as a sacrifice. Just as the blade was about to come down, God stepped in and said, 'Stop! I will provide.' Sheikh, nearly two thousand years ago, on a hill very close to where you and I are sitting, God kept that promise and sent his Son. This time, however, the ax did not stop. God offered his Son. I am a follower of this Jesus, and until we receive this Son whom God has sent, we will be offering our sons and daughters in a world of hatred and strife."

Islam is willing to destroy for the sake of its ideology. I want to suggest that the choice we face is really not between religion and secular atheism, as Sam Harris, Richard Dawkins, Christopher Hitchens, and others have positioned it. Secularism simply does not have the sustaining or moral power to stop Islam. Even now, Europe is demonstrating that its secular worldview—one that Harris applauds—cannot stand against the onslaught of

Islam and is already in demise. In the end, America's choice will be between Islam and Jesus Christ. History will prove before long the truth of this contention.

One Boy's Moral Stand

I leave you now, fellow Americans, with a tender story that brings some hope, some love, and some morality back to our lives for all of the right reasons. The story, reported in the *Houston Chronicle* on March 16, 2007, is about an eleven-year-old boy named Roger Holloway. His baby sister was delivered stillborn at thirty-one weeks and would have been disposed of in the usual manner—nameless and unmarked. The "fetus," simply marked "Fetus Girl Holloway," had been held at the Harris County Medical Examiner's office. For one year, young Roger battled with the authorities for the body of the baby he had named Rachel. His mother was in a drug rehabilitation facility miles away, the baby's father was unknown, and Roger's own father was dead. But this little guy fought long and hard, speaking to the powers that be and even getting a nearby church to donate a burial plot. And on March 15, 2007, Roger and his three cousins held the funeral and carried the white casket to its resting place. In the casket containing Rachel's body he placed a baby blanket, flowers, and stuffed animals.

"Since my dad died, I never got to know him," the boy said after the graveside service. "And since my sister died, I never got to know her either. The good thing is she's with God and my dad in heaven, and she's going to rest in peace."

The impact of this little boy was enormous. Hearing what he had done, his mother told her son by telephone that she was proud of him and asked for his forgiveness, and a bereavement counselor who helped Roger achieve his goal said, "I think this is amazing. I'm looking at greatness."

It is because of the values and the heart of a little boy such as Roger that I have hope in the future. I wish Sam Harris and those who write as he does would join me in celebrating such courage and values—and that we would have a better world as a result.

With my prayers for a world of reasonable faith,

RAVI ZACHARIAS
Atlanta, Georgia

NOTES

Page 14: **"published the first of two books"**: *The End of Faith: Religion, Terror, and the Future of Reason* (New York: Norton, 2004); *Letter to a Christian Nation* (New York: Knopf, 2006).

Page 16: **"if he had a magic wand"**: See Bethany Saltman, "The Temple of Reason," *The Sun* 369 (September 2006): 6, *http://www.thesunmagazine.org/369_Harris.pdf* (accessed August 29, 2007).

Page 23: **"makes me embarrassed"**: This statement is part of Ruse's endorsement for Alister McGrath and Joanna Collicutt McGrath's *The Dawkins Delusion? Atheist Fundamentalism and the Denial of the Divine* (London: SPCK, 2007), *http://www.amazon.com/Dawkins-Delusion-Atheist-Funda mentalism-Denial/dp/product-description/083083446X* (accessed August 29, 2007).

Page 23: **Scott Atran**: Scott Atran, November 29, 2006, in "The Reality Club, An Edge Discussion of 'Beyond Belief, Science, Religion, Reason and Survival,'" Edge, *http://www. edge.org/discourse/bb.html* (accessed August 29, 2007). "Beyond Belief" was a conference at the Salk Institute, La Jolla, California, November 5–7, 2006.

Page 27: **Friedrich Nietzsche**: See Friedrich Nietzsche, *The Gay Science*, trans. Walter Kaufmann (New York: Vintage, 1974), 181; for comments on this, see Walter Kaufmann, *Nietzsche: Philosopher, Psychologist, Antichrist*, 4th ed. (Princeton, N.J.: Princeton Univ. Press, 1975), 96–97.

Page 27: **Albert Camus**: Albert Camus, *The Myth of Sisyphus and Other Essays* (New York: Vintage, 1991), 3.

Page 32: **Bertrand Russell**: For this particular exchange between Copleston and Russell, see Al Seckel, ed., *Bertrand Russell on God and Religion* (Buffalo, N.Y.: Prometheus, 1986), 138–39. A transcript of this debate is available online; see *http://www.bringyou.to/apologetics/p20.htm* (accessed September 17, 2007). This conversation appears under the heading "The Argument from Contingency."

Page 33: **Stephen Jay Gould**: Quoted in David Friend and the editors of *Life* magazine, *The Meaning of Life* (Boston: Little, Brown and Company, 1991), 33.

Page 34: **"Francis Crick's answer"**: Quoted in Michael J. Behe, *Darwin's Black Box: The Biochemical Challenge to Evolution*, 10th anniversary ed. (New York: Free Press, 2006), 248.

Page 34: **"viewing the whole universe"**: Quoted in Philip Graham Ryken, *Jeremiah and Lamentations: From Sorrow to Hope* (Wheaton, Ill.: Crossway, 2001), 100.

Page 34: **Carl Sagan**: See Carl Sagan, "The Quest for Extraterrestrial Intelligence," *Cosmic Search* 1 (1978), *http://www.bigear.org/vol1no2/sagan.htm*.

Page 35: **Donald Page**: Cited in William Lane Craig, "In Defense of Rational Theism," in *Does God Exist? The Great Debate*, ed. J. P. Moreland and Kai Nielsen (Nashville: Nelson, 1990), 143.

Page 35: **"The trouble is"**: Quoted in ibid.

Page 36: **Carl Sagan**: Cited in J. P. Moreland, "Yes! A Defense of Christianity," in *Does God Exist?* 35–36.

Page 37: **C. S. Lewis**: C. S. Lewis, *Miracles* (New York: Macmillan, 1978), 27–28.

Page 41: **"a man left a suicide note"**: Adam Goldman, "The Suicide Capital of America," AP News, February 9, 2004, *http://www.cbsnews.com/stories/2004/02/09/health/main599070.shtml* (accessed September 17, 2007).

Page 43: **Voltaire**: Voltaire, "Poem on the Lisbon Disaster," in *A Treatise on Toleration and Other Essays*, trans. Joseph McCabe (New York: Prometheus, 1994), 1–7.

Page 44: **Antony Flew**: Antony Flew, "The Case for God Challenged," in *Does God Exist?* 167. Flew writes, "[J. P.] Moreland's appeal to his 'personal experiences' strikes me as absolutely grotesque."

Page 44: **"The stars are raining down"**: Quoted in Os Guinness, *Long Journey Home: A Guide to Your Search for the Meaning of Life* (Colorado Springs: WaterBrook, 2001), 33–34.

Page 44: **"I would like and hope I'll die"**: Quoted in Jonathan Dollimore, *Death, Desire and Loss in Western Culture* (New York: Routledge, 1998), 305.

Page 45: **"To die for the love of boys"**: Quoted in Mark Lilla, *The Reckless Mind* (New York: New York Review of Books, 2001), 137–58.

Page 45: **"Foucault's answers to a student"**: Quoted in Guinness, *Long Journey Home*, 35.

Page 51: **"I want to raise a generation"**: Quoted in Jason R. Roberts, "The Search for Absolute Truth in a Secularized Society," *Think*, May 2007, 9, *http://www.focuspress.org/blog/?p=9* (accessed September 5, 2007).

Page 53: **"I do not know the solution"**: Bertrand Russell, letter to the editor, *Observer* (London), October 6, 1957.

Page 54: **"I don't have any justification"**: For this particular exchange between Copleston and Russell, see Seckel, ed., *Bertrand Russell on God and Religion*, 138–39; a transcript of this debate can be viewed at *http://www.bringyou.to/ apologetics/p20.htm*. This conversation appears under the heading "The Moral Argument."

Page 56: **J. L. Mackie**: Quoted in J. P. Moreland, "Reflections on Meaning in Life without God," *Trinity Journal* NS9 (1988): 14.

Page 57: **Kai Nielsen**: Kai Nielsen, "Why Should I Be Moral?" *American Philosophical Quarterly* 21 (1984): 90.

Page 62: **"We are living now"**: Aldous Huxley, *Ends and Means* (London: Chatto & Windus, 1946), 310.

Page 62: **Richard Dawkins**: See Richard Dawkins, *A Devil's Chaplain* (London: Weidenfield & Nicholson, 2003), 34.

Page 62: **Michael Polanyi**: See Michael Polanyi, *Science, Faith, and Society* (Chicago: Univ. of Chicago Press, 1946); also his *Personal Knowledge: Towards a Post-Critical Philosophy* (Chicago: Univ. of Chicago Press, 1962); see also Philip Lewin, "The Problem of Objectivity in Post-critical Philosophy," *http://www.missouriwestern.edu/orgs/polanyi/TAD%20 WEB%20ARCHIVE/TAD18-1/TAD18-1-fnl-pg18-26-pdf.pdf* (accessed September 18, 2007).

Page 63: **Viktor Frankl**: Viktor E. Frankl, *The Doctor and the Soul: From Psychotherapy to Logotherapy* (New York: Vintage, 1973), xxi.

Page 63: **Abdurrahman Wahid**: See Bret Stephens, "The Last King of Java," *Wall Street Journal*, April 7, 2007, A9.

Page 66: **"suffers from a rare malady"**: See "Rare Nerve Disorder Leaves Girl Pain-free," AP News, April 26, 2004, *http://www.msnbc.msn.com/id/4788525/* (accessed September 7, 2007); Steve Sternberg, "Chronic Pain: The Enemy Within," *USA Today*, May 8, 2005, *http://www.usatoday.com/ news/health/2005-05-08-chronic-pain-cover_x.htm* (accessed September 7, 2007).

Page 67: **O. Hobart Mowrer**: See O. Hobart Mowrer, "Sin, the Lesser of Two Evils," *American Psychologist* 15 (1960): 301–4.

Page 69: **Karl Marx**: Karl Marx, "A Contribution to the Critique of Hegel's Philosophy of Right," in *Early Writings*, trans. Rodney Livingstone (London: Penguin, 1975), 244.

Page 69: **"dancing to one's DNA"**: See Richard Dawkins, *River out of Eden* (New York: Basic Books, 1995), 133.

Page 71: **Bertrand Russell**: See Bertrand Russell, *The Autobiography of Bertrand Russell*, vol. 1 (London: George Allen and Unwin, 1967), 13.

Page 71: **"true story of Geary and Mary Jean"**: See Patricia Edmonds, "Crash Took Devoted Parents, Loving Children," *USA Today*, September 27, 1993, A3.

Page 72: **"A pig is of more value"**: See Peter Singer, "Sanctity of Life or Quality of Life," *Pediatrics* (July 1983), 129.

Page 76: **"The obvious inference"**: Scott Atran, November 29, 2006, in "The Reality Club: An Edge Discussion," *http://www.edge.org/discourse/bb.html* (accessed August 29, 2007).

Page 79: **"conversation with author and pastor"**: See "God Debate: Sam Harris vs. Rick Warren," *Newsweek*, April 9, 2007, *http://www.msnbc.msn.com/id/17889148/site/newsweek/* (accessed September 18, 2007).

Page 81: **"are many questionable assumptions"**: Sam Harris, "The Empty Wager," in the online column *On Faith: A Conversation on Religion with Jon Meacham and Sally Quinn*, *http://newsweek.washingtonpost.com/onfaith/sam_harris /2007/04/the_cost_of_betting_on_faith.html* (accessed October 1, 2007).

Page 95: **"Carolyn Porco's suggestion"**: See Scott Atran, November 29, 2006, in "The Reality Club: An Edge Discussion," *http://www.edge.org/discourse/bb.html* (accessed August 29, 2007). Atran comments, "We heard from Carolyn Porco that science education, pure reasoning about existential problems such as death, and collective rituals to replace religious awe with the awe and wonder of science may help free us from religion and religious violence.... 19th century French positivists proposed very much what Dr. Porco proposes in terms—albeit somewhat tongue in cheek—of awe-inspiring ceremonies and even temples to science. Apart from the few who founded these practices and artifacts, the attempt failed utterly to woo any significant portion of the general population, or even make further inroads among the scientific community. Most scientists rightly thought these efforts were artificial and absurd. Most religious people thought the same."

Page 97: **"as many as 40 percent"**: See E. J. Larson and L. Witham, "Scientists Are Still Keeping the Faith," *Nature* 386 (1997): 435–36; see also Francis Collins, "Why This Scientist Believes in God," April 6, 2007, *http://www.cnn.com/2007/US/04/03/collins.commentary/index.html* (accessed October 1, 2007).

Page 98: **"Equality is a lie"**: Quoted in Philip Novak, *The Vision of Nietzsche* (London: Vega, 2001), 16.

Page 100: **C. S. Lewis**: C. S. Lewis, *The Great Divorce* (New York: Macmillan, 1946), 69.

Page 100: **George MacDonald**: George MacDonald, *Life Essential: The Hope of the Gospel* (Wheaton, Ill.: Shaw, 1974), 24–25.

Page 100: **Philip Yancey**: Philip Yancey, *I Was Just Wondering* (Grand Rapids: Eerdmans, 1998), 69.

Page 101: **"mockery ... borrowed from"**: Christopher Hitchens, *The Missionary Position* (London: Verso, 1995).

Page 101: **"conversation with Andrew Sullivan"**: Sam Harris, January 23, 2007, in "Is Religion 'Built Upon Lies'?" Beliefnet.com, *http://www.beliefnet.com/story/209/story_20904.html* (accessed October 1, 2007).

Page 104: **F. W. Boreham**: F. W. Boreham, "The Sword of Solomon," in *The Blue Flame* (London: Epworth, 1930), 29.

Page 105: **Richard Dawkins**: Quoted in Chris Floyd, "A Trick of the Light: Richard Dawkins on Science and Religion," *Science and Spirit* 10 (July/August 1999): 24–31, *http://www.science-spirit.org/article_detail.php?article_id=71* (accessed October 1, 2007).

Page 109: **Senator Tom Harkin**: Quoted in Nigel Cameron, "You Were a 'Dot' Once Too," October 19, 2004, *http://www.tothesource.org/10_20_2004/10_20_2004.htm* (accessed September 18, 2007).

Page 112: **"Many leading proponents"**: See, for example, Robert P. George, "The Moral Status of the Human Embryo," *Perspectives in Biology and Medicine* 48 (Spring 2005): 201–10.

Page 112: **Charles Krauthammer**: Charles Krauthammer, "Stem Cell Miracle?" *Washington Post* (January 12, 2007), A19, *http://www.washingtonpost.com/wp-dyn/content/article/2007/01/11/AR2007011101571.html* (accessed October 1, 2007).

Page 112: **"The odds themselves are not"**: Cited in Nigel Cameron and Lori Andrews, "Cloning and the Debate on Abortion," *Chicago Tribune*, August 8, 2001, *http://www.genetics-and-society.org/resources/items/20010808_chicagotribune_cameron.html* (accessed September 18, 2007).

Page 113: **Nigel Cameron**: Ibid.

Page 113: **Judy Norsigian**: Quoted in ibid.

Page 114: **Nigel Cameron**: Nigel Cameron, "The Challenge of the Biotech Century," *Guardian,* May 21, 2005, *http://www.guardian.co.uk/comment/story/0,,1489112,00.html* (accessed October 1, 2007).

Page 115: **"As Sharansky addressed the media"**: See Abraham Rabinovich, "Return of the Native," *Jerusalem Post*, magazine edition, February 7, 1997, 12.

Page 116: **King Crimson**: From "Epitaph," lyrics written by Peter Sinfield, performed by King Crimson, 1969.

Page 116: **"We have found that"**: Quoted in Sir Martin Rees, *Our Final Hour: A Scientist's Warning* (New York: Basic Books, 2003), 42.

Page 116: **"does not throw dice"**: Albert Einstein's letter to Max Born, 12 December 1926, 1926, quoted in Ronald William Clark, *Einstein: The Life and Times* (New York: Avon, 1972).

Page 117: **"you may read it in the book"**: See Dallas Willard, "Language, Being, God, and the Three Stages of Theistic Evidence," in *Does God Exist?* 197–218.

Page 121: **C. S. Lewis**: C. S. Lewis, *The Abolition of Man* (New York: Macmillan, 1947), 48.

Page 126: **John Polkinghorne**: John Polkinghorne, *One World: The Interaction of Science and Theology* (London: SPCK, 1986), 97–98.

Page 128: **"Since my dad died"**: Quoted in Peggy O'Hare, "Boy Gets a Proper Burial for His Stillborn Sister," *Houston Chronicle*, March 16, 2007, B1.

SUBJECT INDEX

A

abortion, 59–60
  and moral value of life,
    106–11
absolute morality, 99
accident, 31
Acts 17:24–28, 124
aesthetic design, 118–19
alienation, 17
Andrews, Lori, 113
answers, ultimate, 41–44
Aristotle, 81
atheism
  atheists and the new
    atheism, 23–24
  author's study of, 29–30
  classification of, 49–50
  and death, 74
  definition of love, 69–72
  and hope, 74
  and morality, 64–65
  no ultimate answers,
    41–44
  as refusal to deny the
    obvious, 47
  starting point of, 32
  taken to logical
    conclusions, 44–46
Atran, Scott, 23, 76

B

belief, 79–80
Bible, 43
  prophecy, 86–88
Big Bang, 31
bomb, 115–16
Boreham, F. W., 103
Buddhism, 89–91, 93, 96

C

Cameron, Nigel, 112–13,
  114
Camus, Albert, 27
caste system, 100
catastrophe, 48
Chancey, Geary and Mary
  Jean, 71

Chesterton, G. K., 39–40
children, exploited, 72, 73
Cho, Seung-Hui, 81
choice, 59
Christianity
    anxiety about sex, 83–84
    Harris's claim of
        superiority of other
        religions, 93
    and slavery, 97–99
CIPA (Congenital
    Insensitivity to Pain
    with Anhidrosis),
    66–67
cloning, human, 103, 111–14
compenetration, 84
Congenital Insensitivity to
    Pain with Anhidrosis
    (CIPA), 66–67
Copleston, Frederick, 54
core ethic, 81
cosmology, 31
creator, 37–38
Crick, Francis, 34
Cupitt, Don, 29

D

Daniel 11, 87
DaVinci Code, The, 64, 78
Dawkins, Richard, 16, 23,
    38, 65, 105
death, 26, 66, 74
depravity, 68
design, aesthetic, 118–19
despair, 28, 40
determinism, 38
disappointment, 41
discrimination, 100

diversity, 123–27
divorce, 99
DNA, 35
Doctor and the Soul, The
    (Frankl), 62–63
Does God Exist? (Willard),
    117
doubt, 59, 101

E

egalitarianism, 98, 99
Einstein, Albert, 31, 116
embryo research, 112
empirical test for belief,
    79–80
emptiness, 17
End of Faith, The (Harris),
    22, 91, 123–24
entity, physical, 117–18
equality, 98
ethic, core, 81
Eucharist, 123–24
evil
    existence of, 55, 56
    and human heart, 68–69
    and pain, 66–67
    relation to existence of
        God, 50–55
evolution, 37, 52
excluded middle, law of, 110
existence
    pointlessness of, 36
    without God, 27
existential test for belief,
    79–80
exploitation, sexual, 72–74
extraterrestrial existence, 36

F

faith, 75–76, 90
felt reality, 66–67
1 Corinthians 11:26, 124
1 Kings
   3:16–28, 103–4
   7:23–28, 87
Flew, Antony, 37, 44
Foucault, Michel, 44–45
Frankl, Viktor, 62–63
free will, 58–59
freedom, 75–76
fundamentalism, 63

G

Gandhi, Mahatma, 92–93,
   100
genetic engineering, 103–5,
   113
George, Robert, 112
Gingras, Gabby, 66–67
Ginsburg, Ruth Bader, 107
God
   argument for existence of,
      56, 117–21
   and death, 66
   denying existence of,
      67–68
   difference from accident,
      31
   evidence of existence, 88
   existence without, 27
   failure to protect
      humanity, 48
   and moral reasoning, 94
   and relation to reality of
      evil, 50–55

God Delusion, The
   (Dawkins), 23
good, 101–102
good, intrinsic, 56
Good Samaritan, 96–97
Gould, Stephen Jay, 32–33,
   45
guruism, 26

H

Hamas, 126
happiness, 48
hardness of human heart, 99
Harkin, Tom, 109
Harris, Sam, 14–18, 21, 22
   and Christ of Scripture,
      82–85
   derision of Mother Teresa,
      101–102
   and Eucharist, 123–24
   and faith, 90
   and genetic engineering,
      103–4
   misunderstanding of
      Pascal's wager, 80–81
   and morality, 46–49
   and origin, 31
   prejudice against Muslims,
      76–77
   and slavery, 97–98
   and stem cell research,
      108–10
   and worship, 94–95
Hawking, Stephen, 31
heart, human, 68–69
   changing, 99–102
Hebrew prophecy, 84
Hinduism, 24, 90, 93

Hitchens, Christopher, 16, 101, 102
Hitler, Adolf, 51–52
Holloway, Roger, 127–28
Holocaust, 50–51, 62, 99
hope, 28, 74–79
hopelessness, 74
Hoyle, Fred, 35
Hume, David, 39
Hurricane Katrina, 48, 50
Huxley, Aldous, 61–62
hypocrisy, 96

I

imaginary time, 31
India, 24, 25–27, 100, 108
individual self, 90–91
infinite nothing, 27
innocents, killing of, 57–58
Institute for Advanced Science, 35
intelligence, 36–37, 118–20
intrinsic good, 56
intrinsic worth, 53, 55, 56, 58
Isaiah, 84–85
  7:14, 82
  8:3, 84–85
  9:6, 85
Islam, 63, 76, 122–23, 126–27

J

Jainism, 92–93
Jeremiah 19:4, 86
Jesus
  in the course of human events, 120–21
  method for changing human hearts, 99–102
  and nature of reality, 28
  resurrection of, 74–75
  in Scripture, 82–85
  and slavery, 99
  teachings about hope, 78
  teachings about worship, 95–96
Job 31:13–15, 98
John, 83–84
justice, ultimate, 80–82

K

Keirstead, Hans, 110–11
killing, 57–58
Kilner, John, 111
King, Martin Luther, Jr., 92
knowledge, 63
Krauthammer, Charles, 112

L

Last Temptation of Christ, The, 64, 78
law of the excluded middle, 110
lawgiver, moral, 55–56
Letter to a Christian Nation (Harris), 14–18, 21, 22, 46–49
Lewis, C. S., 37, 100, 121
life
  beginning of, 34
  innocent, 58
  intrinsic worth of, 53
  moral value of, 106–11
  random, 34–37
  without purpose, 41

loneliness, 40–41
love, 59
  definition of, 69–72
  mother's, 70–71
  sacrificial, 71–72
  as way to change human
    hearts, 99
Luke 10:25–37, 96

M

MacDonald, George, 100
Mackie, J. L., 56
Mahavira, 92
Marx, Karl, 68–69
Mary Magdalene, 78
mathematics, 105
Matthew, 86
  4:3, 6, 9, 88
  19:8, 99
  22:37, 39, 96
  27:9–10, 86
meaning, 39–46, 61
meaninglessness, 17
memes, 38
Miracles (Lewis), 37
Missionary Position, The
    (Hitchens), 101
moral framework, 57–58
moral lawgiver, 55–56
moral order, 52, 60–63
moral reasoning, 46, 81, 94
moral value, 106–11
morality, 26, 46–74
  absolute, 99
  and atheists, 64–65
  and moral lawgiver, 55–56
  objective, 54
  and redemption, 94

and Ten Commandments,
    93–97
Mother Teresa, 101–2
mother's love, 70–71
Mowrer, O. Hobart, 67
Muggeridge, Malcolm, 39,
    68
Muslims, 76–78
"Myth of Sisyphus, The"
    (Camus), 27

N

natural selection, 52, 72
New Orleans, 48, 50
Nielsen, Kai, 57
Nietzsche, Friedrich, 26–27,
    98
Norsigian, Judy, 113
nothing
  infinite, 27
  relation to something,
    32–34, 118

O

objective morality, 54
oblivion, 26
*One World: The Interaction
    of Science and Theology*
    (Polkinghorne), 31,
    124–26
origin, 31–38
Oxford University, 65

P

Padmasambhava, 89
Page, Donald, 35
pain, 39–41, 66–67
partial birth abortion, 107
Pascal's wager, 79–81

Paul, 83
physical entity, 117–18
pleasure, 39–41
    fleeting, 80–82
    without boundaries, 41, 82
Polanyi, Michael, 62
Polkinghorne, John, 31,
    124–26
Porco, Carolyn, 95
pornography, 73
prejudice, 77
prophecy
    Hebrew, 84
    nature of, 86–88
punishment, 100
purpose, 26, 32, 41

R

racism, 100
radical secularism, 122–23
random life, 34–37
reality
    felt, 66–67
    nature of, 28
reason, 37–38
    as provider of moral
        framework, 57–58
reasoning, moral, 46, 94
redemption, 94
relativity, 31
religion, 25–27
    comparisons, 120
    and radical secularism,
        122–23
    and science, 124
Revelation 5:9, 124
righteousness, 94, 100
RNA, 35

Ross, Hugh, 59
Ruse, Michael, 23
Russell, Bertrand, 32,
    52–54, 71, 92–93, 116

S

sacrificial love, 71–72
Sagan, Carl, 34, 36
Sakharov, Andrei, 115
Sartre, Jean-Paul, 39, 43
science
    and moral decisions, 106
    moral incapacity of, 61–62
    and religion, 124
2 Chronicles 4:2–5, 87
secularism, 122–23, 126–27
self
    and Buddhism, 89–91
    individual, 90–91
self-fulfillment, 79
Selfish Gene, The (Dawkins),
    38
sensual bankruptcy, 82
Serrano, Andres, 64
sex, anxiety about, 83–84
sexual exploitation, 72–74
Sharansky, Natan, 115
significance, 36
Singer, Peter, 72, 107
slavery, 97–99
Solomon, 103–4
something
    relation to nothing,
        32–34, 118
special pleading, 90
specificity, intelligent,
    118–19
stem cells, 107, 109, 110–11

suffering, 15, 48, 58–59
suicide, 16, 27–28
Sullivan, Andrew, 101
supernatural, 24
survival of the fittest, 52
"Sword of Solomon, The"
    (Boreham), 103

T
Ten Commandments, 93–97
theism, Christian, 37
thirty silver coins, 86
time, imaginary, 31
transcending value, 56
trust, 59
truth, 115–16, 117

U
ultimate answers, 41–44
ultimate justice, 80–82
unity, 123–27

V
value
    intrinsic, 58
    of life, 106–11
    transcending, 56
violence, 64
virgin birth, 72–73, 83–85

Virginia Tech University,
    81, 91
"Viruses of the Mind"
    (Dawkins), 38
Voltaire, 42–43, 52

W
Wahid, Abdurrahman, 63
Warren, Rick, 79
Wickramasinghe, N. C., 35
Wilde, Oscar, 40
Willard, Dallas, 117
women, 72, 73, 79
world ensemble cosmology,
    31
world religions, 25–27
worldview, 30–31
worship, 94–95
worth
    intrinsic, 53, 55, 56, 58
    transcending, 56

Y
Yamanaka, Shinya, 111
Yancey, Philip, 100
Z
Zacharias, Ravi
    introduction to, 23–30
Zechariah 11:12, 86

Share Your Thoughts

With the Author: Your comments will be forwarded to the author when you send them to *zauthor@zondervan.com*.

With Zondervan: Submit your review of this book by writing to *zreview@zondervan.com*.

Free Online Resources at
www.zondervan.com/hello

 Zondervan AuthorTracker: Be notified whenever your favorite authors publish new books, go on tour, or post an update about what's happening in their lives.

 Daily Bible Verses and Devotions: Enrich your life with daily Bible verses or devotions that help you start every morning focused on God.

 Free Email Publications: Sign up for newsletters on fiction, Christian living, church ministry, parenting, and more.

 Zondervan Bible Search: Find and compare Bible passages in a variety of translations at www.zondervanbiblesearch.com.

 Other Benefits: Register yourself to receive online benefits like coupons and special offers, or to participate in research.